Scotland's leading educational publishers

Practice Papers for SQA Exams

National 5

© 2014 Leckie & Leckie Ltd
Cover © ink-tank and associates/Muzhik

001/13012014

10 9 8 7 6 5 4 3 2 1

ISBN 9780007504978

Published by
Leckie & Leckie Ltd
An imprint of HarperCollins*Publishers*
Westerhill Road, Bishopbriggs, Glasgow, G64 2QT
T: 0844 576 8126   F: 0844 576 8131
leckieandleckie@harpercollins.co.uk   www.leckieandleckie.co.uk

Special thanks to
Ruth Hall (proofread); Ink Tank (cover design);
QBS (layout and illustrations)

Printed in Italy by Lego, S.P.A.

A CIP Catalogue record for this book is available from the British Library.

Acknowledgements
All images © Shutterstock.com

Whilst every effort has been made to trace the copyright holders, in cases where this has been unsuccessful, or if any have inadvertently been overlooked, the Publishers would gladly receive any information enabling them to rectify any error or omission at the first opportunity.

Introduction

Layout of the Book

This book contains practice exam papers, which mirror the actual SQA exam as much as possible. The layout, paper colour and question level are similar to the actual exam that you will sit, so that you are familiar with what the exam paper will look like.

The answer section is at the back of the book. The answers include practical tips on how to tackle certain types of questions, details of how marks are awarded and advice on what the examiners will be looking for. You will also find that we have included some additional answers that are not mentioned in the topic index to help you with your revision, e.g. the formation of stalactites and stalagmites is given alongside the answer for limestone pavement in question 2b in Exam C.

Revision advice is provided in this introductory section of the book.

How To Use This Book

The practice papers can be used in two main ways:

1. You can complete an entire practice paper as preparation for the final exam. If you would like to use the book in this way, you can complete the practice paper under exam style conditions by setting yourself a time for each paper and answering it as well as possible without using any references or notes. Alternatively, you can answer the practice paper questions as a revision exercise, using your notes to produce a model answer. Your teacher may mark these for you.

2. You can use the Topic Index to find all the questions within the book that deal with a specific topic. This allows you to focus specifically on areas that you particularly want to revise or, if you are mid-way through your course, it lets you practise answering exam-style questions for just those topics that you have studied.

The Exam

Listed below is an outline of the topics assessed in the National 5 Geography Exam. You can obtain a detailed course outline from the SQA website at sqa.org.uk or ask your teacher for a copy.

The exam is divided into three sections:

1. Physical Environments

- Weather – the effect of latitude, relief, aspect and distance from sea on local weather conditions; the characteristics of the five main air masses affecting the UK; the characteristics of weather associated with depressions and anticyclones

- Landscapes formation — **either** Glaciated Uplands and Coastal Landscapes **or** Upland Limestone and Rivers and Valleys

- Land uses including farming, forestry, industry, recreation and tourism, water storage and supply and renewable energy

- Land use conflicts and solutions

2. Human Environments

In relation to developing and developed countries

- Indicators of development

- Population distribution

- Birth rates and death rates

In relation to urban areas

- Land use zones in cities in the developed world

- Recent developments in the CBD, inner city, rural/urban fringe in developed world cities

- Issues/Solutions in developing world cities

In relation to rural areas

- Changes/modern developments to farming in developed countries

- Changes/modern developments to farming in developing countries

3. Global Issues

Candidates should study at least **two** global issues from the following:

Climate change

- Features of climate change

- Physical and human causes of climate change

- Local and global effects

- Managing and reducing its impact/effects

Impact of human activity on the natural environment

- Tundra and equatorial climates and their ecosystems

- Uses and misuses of these areas

- Effects of degradation on people and the environment

- Managing and reducing its impact/effects

Environmental hazards

- The main features of earthquakes, volcanoes and tropical storms

- Causes of each hazard

- Impact on the landscape and population of each hazard

- Management – methods of prediction, planning and strategies adopted in response to environmental hazards

Trade and globalisation

- Patterns of world trade

- Cause of inequalities in trade

- Impact of world trade patterns on people and the environment

- Methods to reduce inequalities — trade alliances, fair trade, sustainable practices

Tourism

- Mass tourism and eco-tourism

- Causes of/reasons for mass tourism and eco-tourism

- Effect of mass tourism and eco-tourism on people and the environment

- Methods adopted to manage tourism

Health

- Distribution of selected world diseases

- Causes, effects and methods adopted to manage:
  - AIDS in developed and developing countries
  - one disease prevalent in a developed country (choose from: heart disease, cancer, asthma)
  - one disease prevalent in a developing country (choose from: malaria, cholera, kwashiorkor, pneumonia)

Skills

Skills will be assessed across the three areas. Ordnance Survey (OS) mapping skills will be assessed in the Physical Environments and Human Environments units. Handling, extracting and interpreting information from graphs, tables and statistics will be assessed in all three units.

General Information about the exam

You have 1 hour 30 minutes to complete the paper.

There are three sections with each section worth 20 marks – 60 marks in total.

Section 1 — Physical Environments — 20 marks

In this section you have a choice!

Attempt **EITHER** question 1 **OR** question 2, **AND** questions 3, 4 and 5.

You will have studied two landscape types, **either** Glaciated Uplands and Coastal Landscapes **or** Upland Limestone and Rivers and Valleys. Make sure you choose the correct topic you have studied. Do not attempt to answer both question 1 and 2. **If you answer question 1 do not answer question 2.**

Section 2 — Human Environments — 20 marks

Attempt all the questions in this section – questions 6, 7 and 8.

Section 3 — Global Issues — 20 marks

In this section you have a choice!

There are six questions. You should attempt any **TWO** of the following; **do not answer all the questions.**

Question 9: Climate Change

Question 10: Impact of Human Activity on the Natural Environment

Question 11: Environmental Hazards

Question 12: Trade and Globalisation

Question 13: Tourism

Question 14: Health

Make sure you choose the topics you have studied!

The Exam Paper

Always check you have the correct paper before you begin the exam.

Complete your exam in either blue or black ink. Always make sure you have a spare pen in case one runs out. A pencil is useful for diagrams.

Answering the Questions

You can answer the questions in whatever order you feel comfortable with but remember to clearly identify the question number you are attempting.

Carefully read each question so you answer what the question is asking. Put as much detail into your answer as possible – detail will gain you marks.

In questions that ask you to explain the formation of a feature, e.g. a corrie, it is possible to gain full marks by producing a series of diagrams. To do this you should add labels with explanations for your diagrams.

Do not use bullet points or lists, you should answer in sentences. The examiner is looking for you to show your knowledge of the course topics and a simple list is too basic and will not gain you full marks for the question.

Always attempt a question. Even if you are not sure of the answer you may pick up a few marks for your attempt.

There will be OS map questions. These questions could come up in the Physical section, the Human section, or both.

There will probably be more than one OS map. Maps will have item letters, e.g. Item A, Item B etc. The question will clearly state which map to use by indicating the item letter. There may be a different map used in the Physical section from the Human section – make sure you select the correct map. In OS questions always give evidence from the map, e.g. if you are asked for evidence to show the CBD of an area don't just use your knowledge to state the features of a CBD – you need to give actual examples from the OS map. Also, at National 5 you will be expected to use six figure grid references, although in some cases four figures will be sufficient.

There are six types of question used in these practice papers.

1. Describe	This is basically a list of facts. No reasons are needed in your answer.
	Example: **Describe** the location of an out of town shopping centre.
	Answer: It is found on the edge of town. There is plenty of housing close by. There are large areas of flat land with roads nearby.
2. Explain and	This means you have to give reasons to support your answer using words like 'because', 'which means that', 'since' and 'as'.
3. Give reasons	**Below is the same question but answered as an explanation.**
	Example: **Explain** the location of an out of town shopping centre.
	Answer: It is found on the outskirts of a town **because** there is plenty of room to expand. There is housing close by so that **means that** there are customers to buy the goods from the shopping centre. The housing **means that** there will be a labour force available for the shopping centre. The areas of flat land **means** it is easier to build on and there is plenty of land for car parking **as** most customers will arrive by car. There are roads nearby **which means that** goods can be transported in and out. **Since** more people will arrive by car the roads nearby make the area more accessible.

4. Match	In this type of question you will be asked to use your OS skills to match grid references to specific items.
	Example: **Match** the following grid references to the correct feature
	Grid References 367198, 673056, 234875
	Choose from: forestry, quarry, loch, A124
5. Give map evidence	This means you have to use map evidence in your answer. You need to pick out specific features from the map.
	Example: **Give map evidence** to show that the CBD of Dunfermline is found in grid square 378695
	Answer: There are many churches. There are museums. There is a town hall. There is tourist information. All the transport routes meet in this square.
6. Give advantages and disadvantages	In this type of question you need to evaluate the good and bad points of a particular situation.
	Example: **Give the advantages and disadvantages** of deforestation.
	Answer: Advantages: The trees can be exported to make money for the country. The extraction of timber provides jobs for the people. The money for the trees can be used to improve the lives of the local people.
	Disadvantages: The trees are the habitat of many species of birds and animals which could become extinct. The native tribes are forced from their homes and their traditional way of life threatened. Soil erosion occurs as there are no tree roots to bind the soil together.

Timing is important. Each section is worth 20 marks so you should aim to complete each section in about 25 minutes. This should give you time to read the questions, make your selection in the choice section and leave you enough time to look over your paper at the end. Do not leave the exam before the end. It should take the whole time allocated to complete your paper. If you have finished well before the end of the exam then you need to go back and put more detail into your answers or attempt unanswered questions.

Your Course award

The National 5 Course has two parts – a question paper (exam) and an assignment.

The question paper will be worth 60 marks and the assignment will have 20 marks. Your mark for the exam and the assignment will be combined to give you a mark out of 80. The question paper is therefore worth 75% of the overall marks for the Course assessment and the assignment is worth 25%.

Course assessment will provide the basis for grading attainment in the Course award.

The Course assessment is graded A–D. The grade is determined on the basis of the total mark for all Course assessments together.

Good luck!

Topic Index

Topic Index	Sub-topic	Exam A	Exam B	Exam C	Knowledge for Prelim			Knowledge for SQA Exam		
					Having difficulty	Still needs work	Okay	Having difficulty	Still needs work	Okay
Mapwork	Matching coastal features on an OS map	Q1a								
	Matching river features on an OS map	Q2a	Q2a							
	Land use cross-section	Q3								
	Adv/dis of shopping centre	Q6a								
	Matching glaciated features		Q1a	Q1a						
	Matching limestone features			Q2a						
	Land use urban fringe	Q6a								

Topic Index	Sub-topic	Exam A	Exam B	Exam C	Knowledge for Prelim			Knowledge for SQA Exam		
					Having difficulty	Still needs work	Okay	Having difficulty	Still needs work	Okay
Mapwork	Physical landscape		Q3	Q3						
	Features of CBD			Q6a						
	Urban environment			Q6b						
Coasts	Headland formation	Q1b								
	Caves, arches and stacks*									
Rivers	V-shaped valley/Ox-bow lake formation*	Q2b								
	Waterfall/U-shaped valley formation*		Q2b								
Glaciation	Corrie/arête formation		Q1b	Q1b						
Limestone	Pavement formation			Q2b						

* Extra answer for this feature is included in worked answers

Topic Index	Sub-topic	Exam A	Exam B	Exam C	Knowledge for Prelim			Knowledge for SQA Exam		
					Having difficulty	Still needs work	Okay	Having difficulty	Still needs work	Okay
Weather	Weather conditions and maps	Q4								
	Synoptic charts comparison		Q4							
	High pressure systems			Q4						
Landscapes	Conflicts and solutions	Q5	Q5							
	Land use suitability			Q5						
	Life expectancy map		Q6a							
Population	Differences in life expectancy		Q6b							
	Demographic transition model	Q7								

Topic Index	Sub-topic	Exam A	Exam B	Exam C	Knowledge for Prelim			Knowledge for SQA Exam		
					Having difficulty	Still needs work	Okay	Having difficulty	Still needs work	Okay
Population	Population pyramids		Q7							
	Development indicators			Q7						
	Population growth			Q8a						
	Population policies			Q8b						
Urban	CBD	Q8								
	Rural fringe		Q8								
Farming	Input changes	Q6b								
	Skills	Q9a	Q9a	Q9a						
Climate Change	Causes of climate change	Q9b								
	Effects of global warming		Q9b								

Topic Index	Sub-topic	Exam A	Exam B	Exam C	Knowledge for Prelim			Knowledge for SQA Exam		
					Having difficulty	Still needs work	Okay	Having difficulty	Still needs work	Okay
Climate Change	Solutions to global warming			Q9b						
	Skills	Q10a	Q10a	Q10a						
Natural Environment	Effects of tundra development	Q10b								
	Methods to reduce the impact of deforestation		Q10b							
	Adv/dis of development of rainforest			Q10b						
Environmental Hazards	Skills	Q11a	Q11a	Q11a						

Topic Index	Sub-topic	Exam A	Exam B	Exam C	Knowledge for Prelim			Knowledge for SQA Exam		
					Having difficulty	Still needs work	Okay	Having difficulty	Still needs work	Okay
Environmental Hazards	Predicting/ managing tropical storms	Q11b								
	Impact of tropical storms		Q11b							
	Impact of an earthquake			Q11b						
	Skills	Q12a	Q12a	Q12a						
Trade and Globalisation	Fair trade	Q12b								
	Trade inequality		Q12b							

Topic Index	Sub-topic	Exam A	Exam B	Exam C	Knowledge for Prelim			Knowledge for SQA Exam		
					Having difficulty	Still needs work	Okay	Having difficulty	Still needs work	Okay
Trade and Globalisation	Cooperatives and fair trade			Q12b						
Tourism	Skills	Q13a	Q13a	Q13a						
	Mass tourism	Q13b								
	Eco-tourism		Q13b							
	Managing tourism			Q13b						
Health	Skills	Q14a	Q14a	Q14a						
	Disease consequences for malaria, heart disease and AIDS	Q14b								
	AIDS management		Q14b							
	Causes of, and responses to, heart disease, malaria, cholera and cancer			Q14b						

Practice Exam A

Practice Exam A

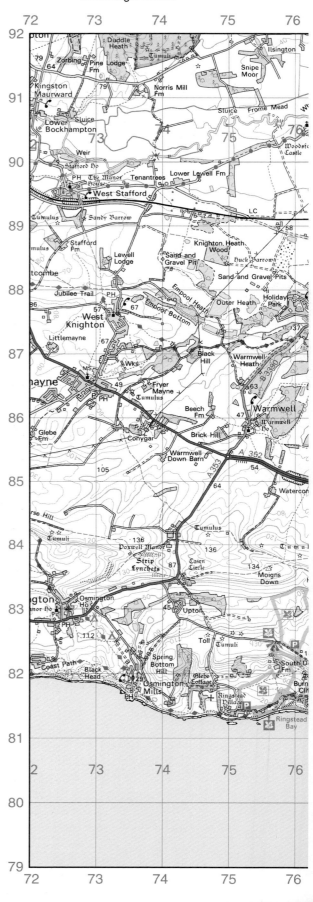

Magnetic North
Grid North
True North

Diagrammatic only

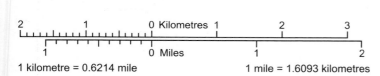

2   1   0 Kilometres 1   2   3

1   0 Miles   1   2

1 kilometre = 0.6214 mile   1 mile = 1.6093 kilometres

Item A: OS map of Wool

Four colours should appear above; if not then please return to the invigilator.

Extract No 1658/194

EXAM A

Total marks — 60

Duration — 1 hour and 30 minutes

SECTION 1 — PHYSICAL ENVIRONMENTS — 20 marks

In this section you must answer: **EITHER** Question 1 **OR** Question 2, **AND** Questions 3, 4 and 5.

SECTION 2 — HUMAN ENVIRONMENTS — 20 marks

In this section you must answer Questions 6, 7 and 8.

SECTION 3 — GLOBAL ISSUES — 20 marks

Answer any **TWO** questions

Question   9 — Climate Change

Question 10 — Impact of Human Activity on the Natural Environment

Question 11 — Environmental Hazards

Question 12 — Trade and Globalisation

Question 13 — Tourism

Question 14 — Health

SECTION 1 — PHYSICAL ENVIRONMENTS

In this section you must answer **EITHER** Question 1 **OR** Question 2, **AND** Questions 3, 4 and 5

Question 1: Coastal Landscapes

See Item A: OS map of Wool

a) Study OS map **Item A** of the Wool area, extract number 1658/194.

Match the coastal features below with the correct grid reference.

bay, stack, headland

822798, 795804, 834796, 807803   **3**

b) **Explain** the formation of a headland.

You may use a diagram(s) to illustrate your answer.   **4**

Total marks 7

NOW ANSWER QUESTIONS 3, 4 AND 5

DO NOT ANSWER THIS QUESTION IF YOU HAVE ALREADY ANSWERED QUESTION 1

Question 2: Rivers and Valleys

See Item A: OS map of Wool

a)   Study OS map **Item A** of the Wool area, extract number 1658/194.

Match the river and valley features shown below with the correct grid reference.

river flowing southeast, meander, ox-bow lake

839875, 813890, 801899, 805880   **3**

b)   **Explain** the formation of a V-shaped valley. You may use a diagram(s) to illustrate your answer.   **4**

Total marks 7

NOW ANSWER QUESTIONS 3, 4 AND 5

MARKS

NOW ANSWER QUESTIONS 3, 4 and 5

Question 3

Diagram Q3A: Location of Transect X – Y

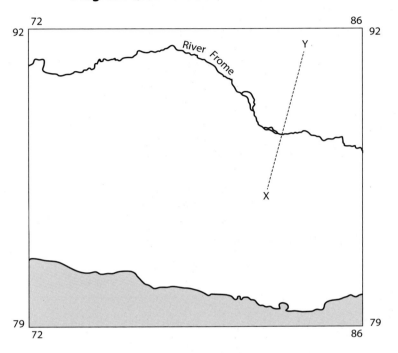

Diagram Q3B: Land Use Across Transect X – Y

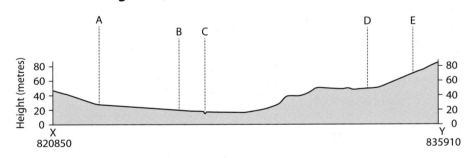

Study OS map **Item A** of the Wool area and Diagrams Q3A and Q3B.

Match the letters shown on Transect X–Y on Diagram Q3B to the correct feature below.

River Frome, A352, coniferous wood, railway, tank training area

4

Question 4

Diagram Q4A: Actual Weather Conditions, 27 November 2012

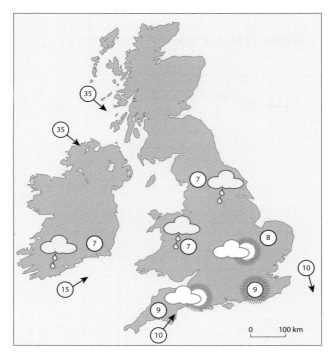

Diagram Q4B: Two Weather Charts for the British Isles, 27 November 2012

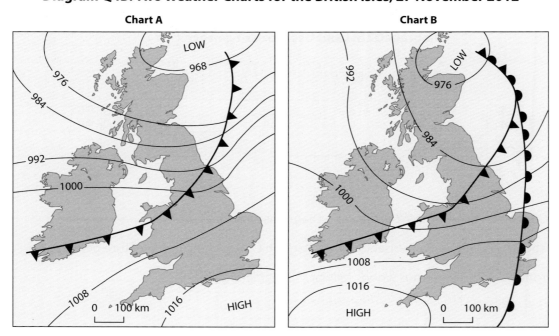

Study Diagrams Q4A and Q4B.

Which weather chart, A or B, is more likely to show the weather conditions being experienced in Diagram Q4A? **Explain** your choice.

4

Question 5

Diagram Q5A: Landscape Types

Glaciated Uplands

Coastal Landscape

Upland Limestone

Rivers and Valleys

Diagram Q5B: Land Use Conflicts

Look at Diagrams Q5A and Q5B.

Choose one landscape that you have studied from Diagram Q5A.

(i) **Describe** one land use conflict from your chosen landscape type and

(ii) **Explain** solutions to your identified conflict.   **5**

SECTION 2 — HUMAN ENVIRONMENTS

In this section you must answer Questions 6, 7 and 8

Question 6

See Item A: OS map of Wool

a) Study OS map **Item A** of the Wool area, extract number 1658/194.

   There is a proposal to build a shopping centre in grid square 7986.

   Using map evidence, give **advantages and/or disadvantages** of this location for a shopping centre. **5**

Diagram Q6B: Inputs in Farming, 1992–2010

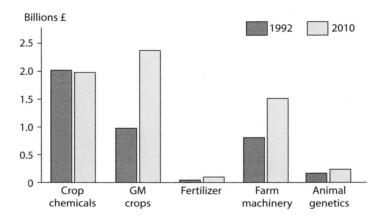

b) Study Diagram Q6B.

   Describe, in detail, the changes in farming inputs between 1992 and 2010. **3**

MARKS

Question 7

Diagram Q7: Demographic Transition Model

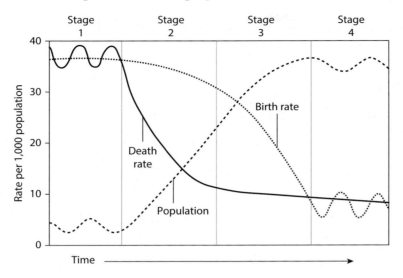

Study Diagram Q7.

Explain the changes in the birth and death rates for **stages 3 and 4** of the Demographic Transition Model.   6

Question 8

Diagram Q8: Features of the CBD

Large
department
stores

Traffic
congestion

Tall/high
density
buildings

Pollution

Main railway/
bus stations

Large number
of pedestrians

Lack of space

Hotels

Look at Diagram Q8.

Explain two features of the CBD.

You should refer to a city you have studied in your answer.

6

SECTION 3 — GLOBAL ISSUES

Answer any TWO questions

Question 9 — Climate Change

Question 10 — Impact of Human Activity on the Natural Environment

Question 11 — Environmental Hazards

Question 12 — Trade and Globalisation

Question 13 — Tourism

Question 14 — Health

Question 9: Climate Change

Diagram Q9: Countries at Risk from Climate Change

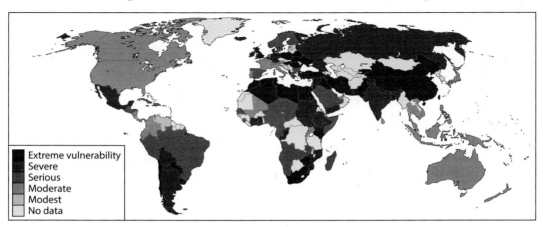

a) Study Diagram Q9.

   Describe, in detail, the extent to which countries are at risk from climate change.   **4**

b) **Explain** the physical **and** human causes of climate change.

   You should refer to examples you have studied in your answer.   **6**

                                                                    Total marks   10

MARKS

Question 10: Impact of Human Activity on the Natural Environment

Diagram Q10: Annual Oil Production in the North Slope, Alaska, 1981–2011

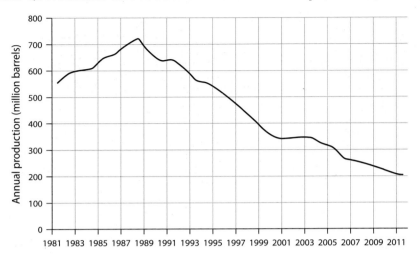

a) Study Diagram Q10.

    Describe, in detail, Alaskan oil production between 1981 and 2011.   **4**

b) For any named area you have studied, **explain, in detail,** the impact of human activities on the people and environment.   **6**

                                                    Total marks 10

Question 11: Environmental Hazards

Diagram Q11A: Earthquakes Greater than Magnitude 7, 1975–2013

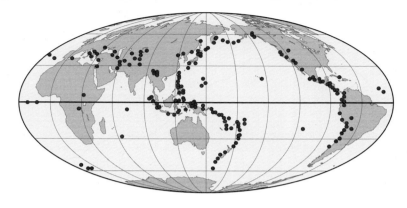

a) Study Diagram Q11A.

Describe, in detail, the distribution of earthquakes greater than magnitude 7 between 1975 and 2013.

4

Diagram Q11B: Tsunami Warning

b) Look at Diagram Q11B.

For an environmental hazard you have studied, **explain** ways in which the effects can be reduced/predicted.

You should refer to examples you have studied in your answer.

6

Total marks 10

Question 12: Trade and Globalisation

Diagram Q12A: World's Largest Economies, 2004–2020 (predicted)

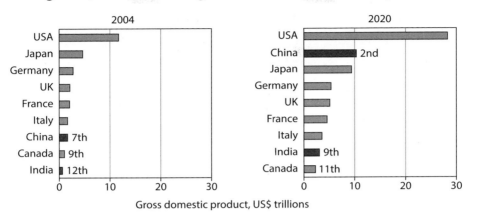

Gross domestic product, US$ trillions

Note: Not shown in 2004: Spain (8th), South Korea (10th) and Mexico (11th)

Not shown in 2020: Russia (8th)

a) Study Diagram Q12A.

   Describe, in detail, the changes in the share of world trade between 2004 and 2020 (predicted).   **4**

Diagram Q12B: Fair Trade

b) Look at Diagram Q12B.

   Explain how fair trade can help improve the lives of people in the developing world.

   You should refer to examples you have studied in your answer.   **6**

Total marks   10

Question 13: Tourism

Diagram Q13A: Growth in International Tourist Arrivals 2010–2011

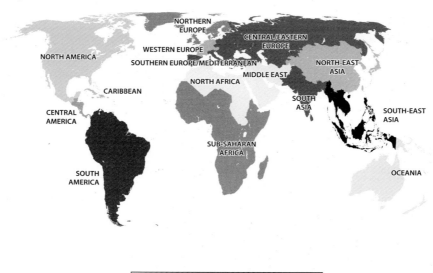

a) Study Diagram Q13A.

Describe, in detail, the growth in international tourist arrivals. **4**

Diagram Q13B: Levante Beach, Benidorm

b) Look at Diagram Q13B.

Explain the advantages **and** disadvantages of mass tourism.

You should refer to examples you have studied in your answer. **6**

Total marks 10

Question 14: Health

Diagram Q14: Causes of Death 2002–2030 (predicted)

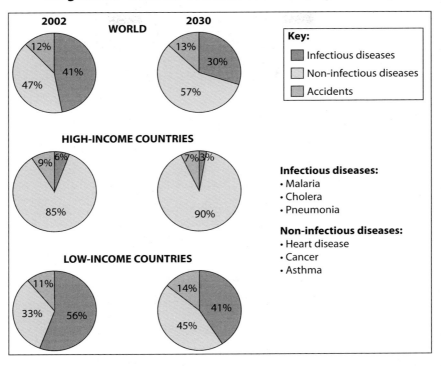

a) Study Diagram Q14.

   Describe the patterns in the causes of death between 2002 and 2030 (predicted).   **4**

b) For a disease you have studied, **explain** the consequences of the disease for the population in an affected area.

   You should refer to examples you have studied in your answer.   **6**

   Total marks 10

[END OF QUESTION PAPER]

Practice Exam B

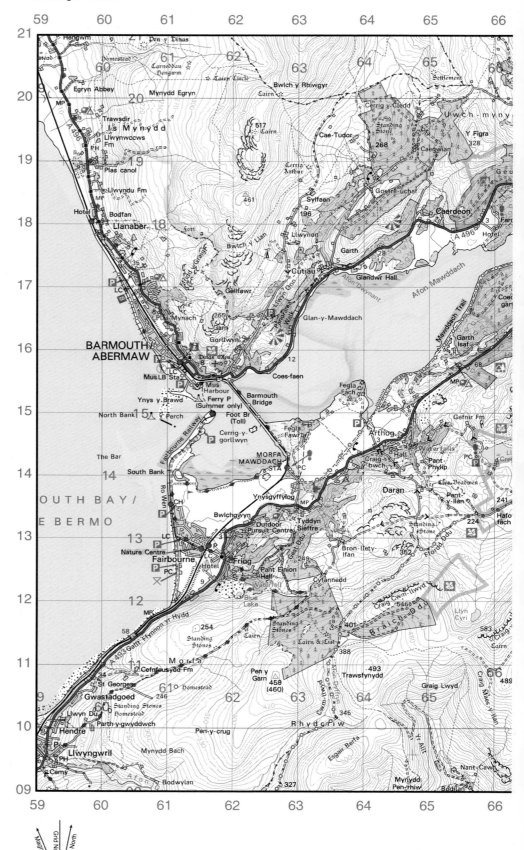

Grid North
Magnetic North
True North

Diagrammatic only

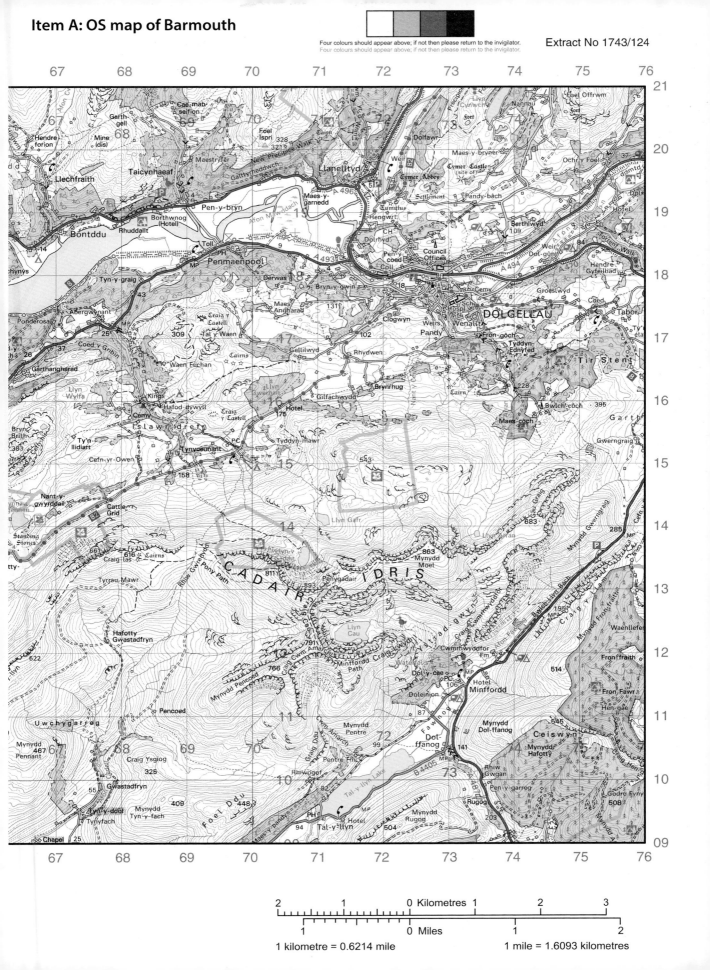

Item A: OS map of Barmouth

Extract No 1743/124

1 kilometre = 0.6214 mile   1 mile = 1.6093 kilometres

EXAM B

Total marks — 60

Duration — 1 hour and 30 minutes

SECTION 1 — PHYSICAL ENVIRONMENTS — 20 marks

In this section you must answer: **EITHER** Question 1 **OR** Question 2, **AND** Questions 3, 4 and 5.

SECTION 2 — HUMAN ENVIRONMENTS — 20 marks

In this section you must answer Questions 6, 7 and 8.

SECTION 3 — GLOBAL ISSUES — 20 marks

Attempt any **TWO** questions

Question 9 — Climate Change

Question 10 — Impact of Human Activity on the Natural Environment

Question 11 — Environmental Hazards

Question 12 — Trade and Globalisation

Question 13 — Tourism

Question 14 — Health

SECTION 1 — PHYSICAL ENVIRONMENTS

In this section you must answer **EITHER** Question 1 **OR** Question 2, **AND** Questions 3, 4 and 5

Question 1: Glaciated Uplands

See Item A: OS map of Barmouth

a) Study OS map **Item A** of the Barmouth area, extract number 1743/124.

Match the glaciated uplands features shown below with the correct grid reference.

U-shaped valley, corrie, arête

706115, 723196, 733110, 713141   3

Diagram Q1: Formation of a Corrie

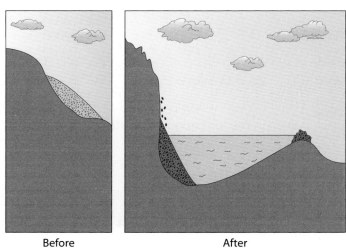

Before   After

b) Look at Diagram Q1.

Explain the processes involved in the formation of a corrie.

You may use diagram(s) in your answer.   4

Total marks   7

NOW ANSWER QUESTIONS 3, 4 AND 5

DO NOT ANSWER THIS QUESTION IF YOU HAVE ALREADY ANSWERED QUESTION 1

Question 2: Rivers and Valleys

See Item A: OS map of Barmouth

a) Study OS map **Item A** of the Barmouth area, extract number 1743/124.

Match the river and valley features shown below with the correct grid reference.

river flowing southwest, V-shaped valley, tributary

715755, 671175, 722200, 738150 **3**

Diagram Q2: Formation of a Waterfall

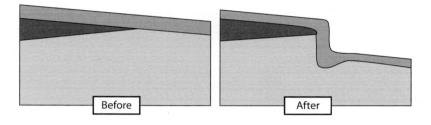

Before   After

b) **Explain** the processes involved in the formation of a waterfall.

You may wish to use a diagram(s) in your answer. **4**

Total marks 7

NOW ANSWER QUESTIONS 3, 4 AND 5

NOW ANSWER QUESTIONS 3, 4 and 5

Question 3

Diagram Q3: The Mawddach Way, Barmouth

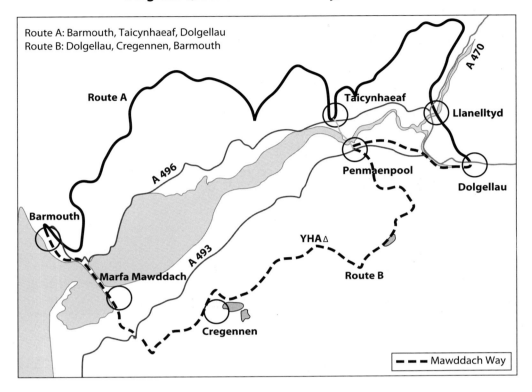

Route A: Barmouth, Taicynhaeaf, Dolgellau
Route B: Dolgellau, Cregennen, Barmouth

Study Diagram Q3 and OS map Item A of the Barmouth area.

A group of walkers have the choice of walking Route A or Route B of the Mawddach Way.

For either Route A or Route B, **describe the advantages and disadvantages** of the route. You must use map evidence in your answer.

5

Question 4

Diagram Q4: Weather Chart UK, August 2012

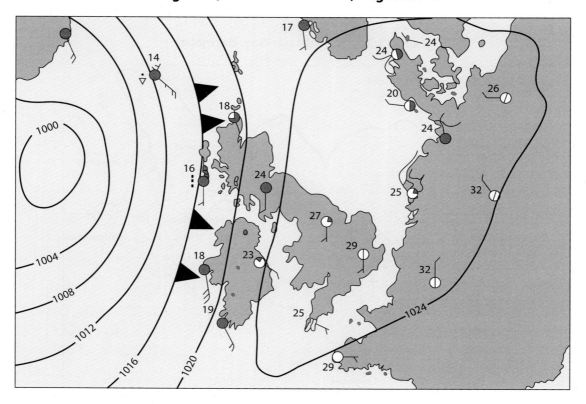

Study Diagram Q4.

Explain the differences in weather conditions between the south of England and the north of Scotland.

4

Question 5

Diagram Q5: Landscape Types and Land Uses

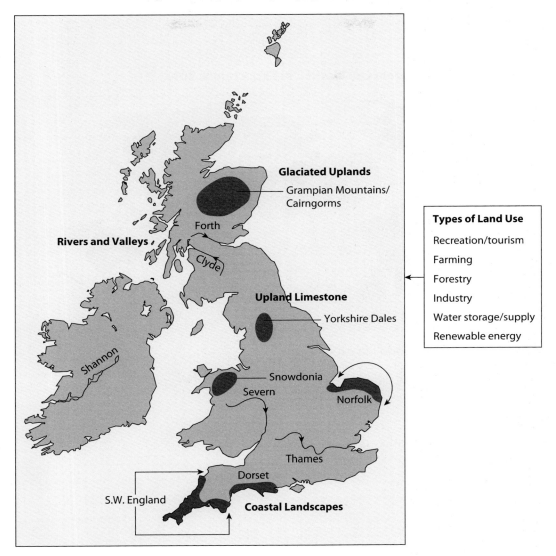

Look at Diagram Q5.

Choose **one** of the landscape types from Diagram Q5 which you have studied.

Explain the conflicts which can arise between any two land uses found in your chosen landscape. **4**

SECTION 2 — HUMAN ENVIRONMENTS

In this section you must answer Questions 6, 7 and 8

Question 6

Diagram Q6: World Life Expectancy, 2012

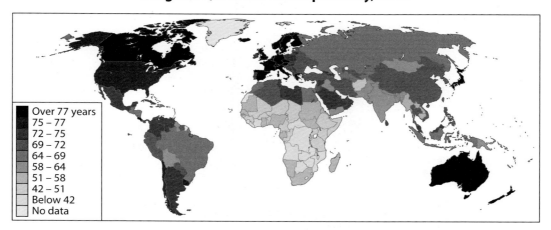

a) Study Diagram Q6.

Describe the pattern of world life expectancy.   4

b) **Explain** the reasons for the differences in life expectancy between developed and developing countries.   6

Question 7

Diagram Q7: Population Pyramids for Scotland

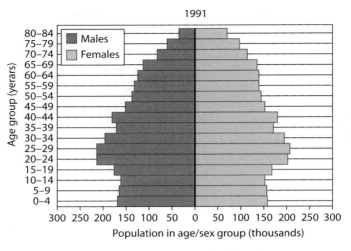

1991

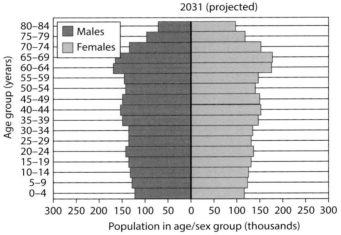

2031 (projected)

Study Diagram Q7.

Describe, in detail, the differences in Scotland's population structure between 1991 and 2031 (projected).

4

Question 8

Diagram Q8: Developments on the Rural/Urban Fringe in the UK

> Out of town shopping centres
>
> Housing
>
> Airport expansion
>
> Retail parks
>
> Hotels and conference centres

Look at Diagram Q8.

Explain the attractions of the rural/urban fringe in the UK for developments like those shown in Diagram Q8.

6

SECTION 3 — GLOBAL ISSUES

Answer any TWO questions

Question   9 — Climate Change

Question 10 — Impact of Human Activity on the Natural Environment

Question 11 — Environmental Hazards

Question 12 — Trade and Globalisation

Question 13 — Tourism

Question 14 — Health

Question 9: Climate Change

Diagram Q9A: Changes in Global Mean Temperatures, 1880–2010

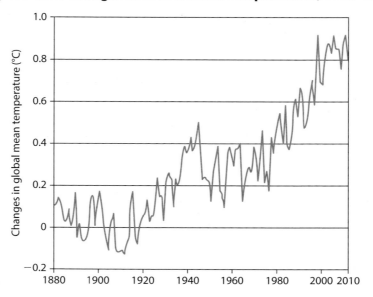

a) Study Diagram Q9A.

   Describe, in detail, the changes in global mean temperatures between 1880 and 2010.   **4**

Diagram Q9B: Effects of Global Warming

b) Look at Diagram Q9B.

   Explain the possible effects of global warming on the environment.   **6**

Total marks 10

Question 10: Impact of Human Activity on the Natural Environment

Diagram Q10: Climate Graphs

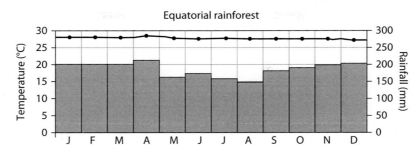

Equatorial rainforest

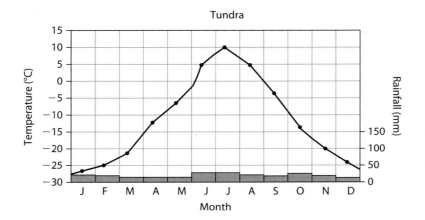

Tundra

a) Study Diagram Q10.

   Describe, in detail, the differences between the climates of the rainforest and tundra shown in the diagram above.　　　　4

b) **Explain, in detail,** strategies used to reduce the impact of deforestation on people and the environment.　　　　6

Total marks　10

Question 11: Environmental Hazards

Diagram Q11: Distribution of Tropical Storms

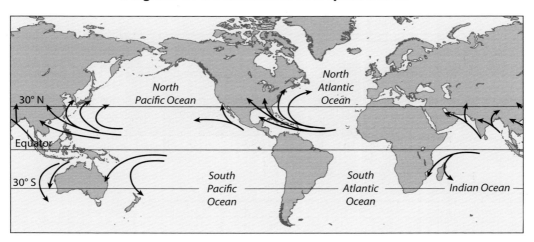

a) Study Diagram Q11.

   Describe, in detail, the distribution of tropical storms.   **4**

b) For a named tropical storm you have studied, **explain** the impact of the storm on the landscape and the population.   **6**

Total marks 10

Question 12: Trade and Globalisation

Diagram Q12A: Growth in Volume of World Trade and GDP, 2005–2013

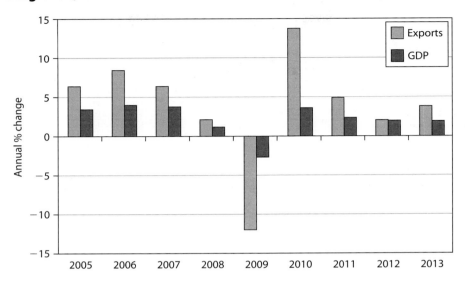

a) Study Diagram Q12A.

Describe, in detail, the changes in the growth of world trade and GDP between 2005 and 2013.

4

Diagram Q12B: Share of World Trade

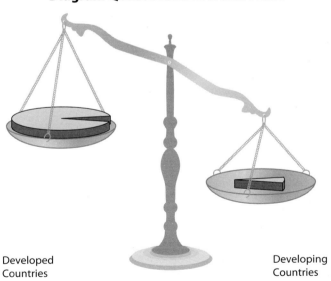

Developed Countries

Developing Countries

b) Look at diagram Q12B.

Explain the reasons for the inequalities in world trade.

6

Total marks   10

Question 13: Tourism

Diagram Q13A: Some Facts on Tourism in California

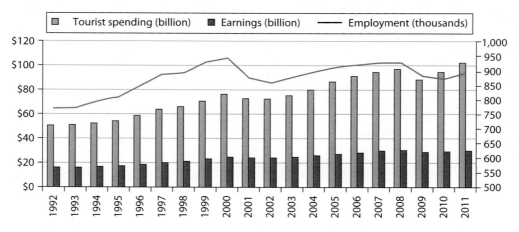

a) Study Diagram Q13A.

 Describe, in detail, the changes in Californian tourism between 1992 and 2011.   **4**

Diagram Q13B: Newspaper Quote

> "The United Nations World Travel Organization estimates that
> in 2012 eco-tourism captured 11% of the international market"

b) Look at the statement above.

 Explain the main features of eco-tourism.   **6**

 Total marks 10

Question 14: Health

Diagram Q14A: Distribution of Child Cases of Pneumonia

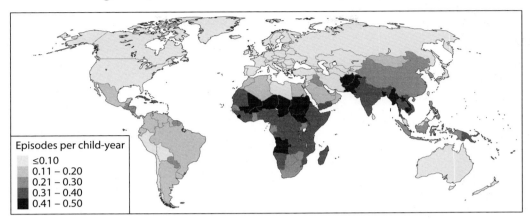

Episodes per child-year
≤0.10
0.11 – 0.20
0.21 – 0.30
0.31 – 0.40
0.41 – 0.50

a) Study Diagram Q14A.

   Describe, in detail, the distribution of child cases of pneumonia.   **4**

Diagram Q14B: AIDS Facts

More than 36 million people live with AIDS/HIV

In 2012, 1.9 million people died from AIDS

Every day nearly 7,000 people contract HIV

b) Look at Diagram Q14B.

   Explain the causes of AIDS and some strategies used to control/manage the disease.   **6**

Total marks   10

[END OF QUESTION PAPER]

Practice Exam C

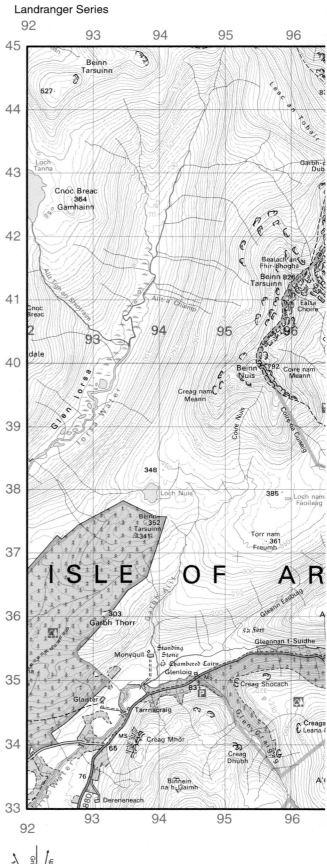

Magnetic North

Grid North

True North

Diagrammatic only

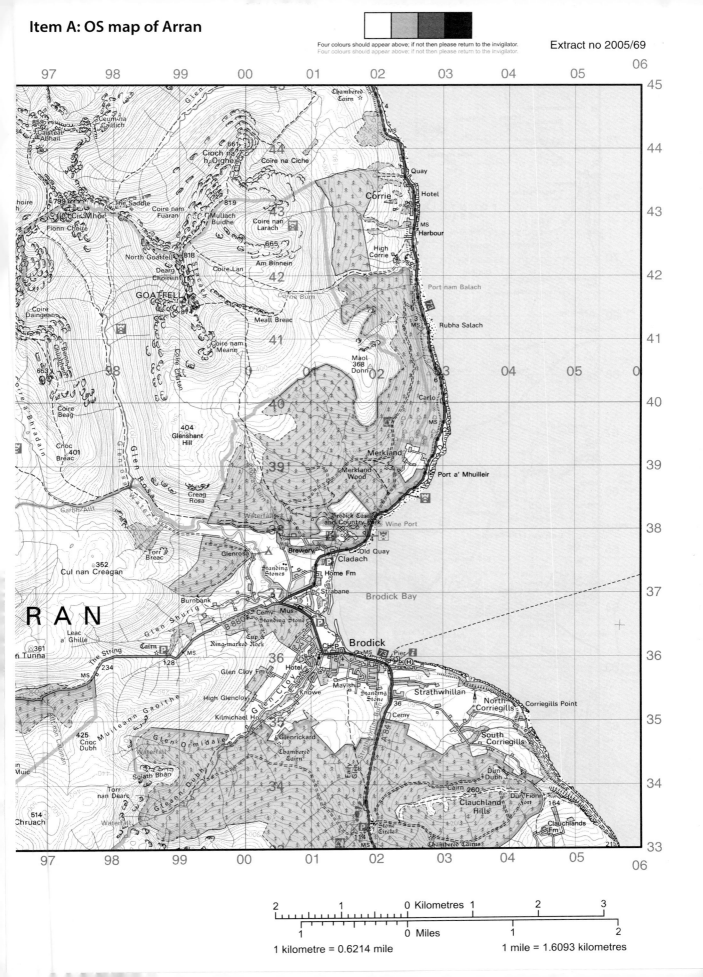

Four colours should appear above; if not then please return to the invigilator.
Four colours should appear above; if not then please return to the invigilator.

Extract no 2005/69

1 kilometre = 0.6214 mile

1 mile = 1.6093 kilometres

Landranger Series

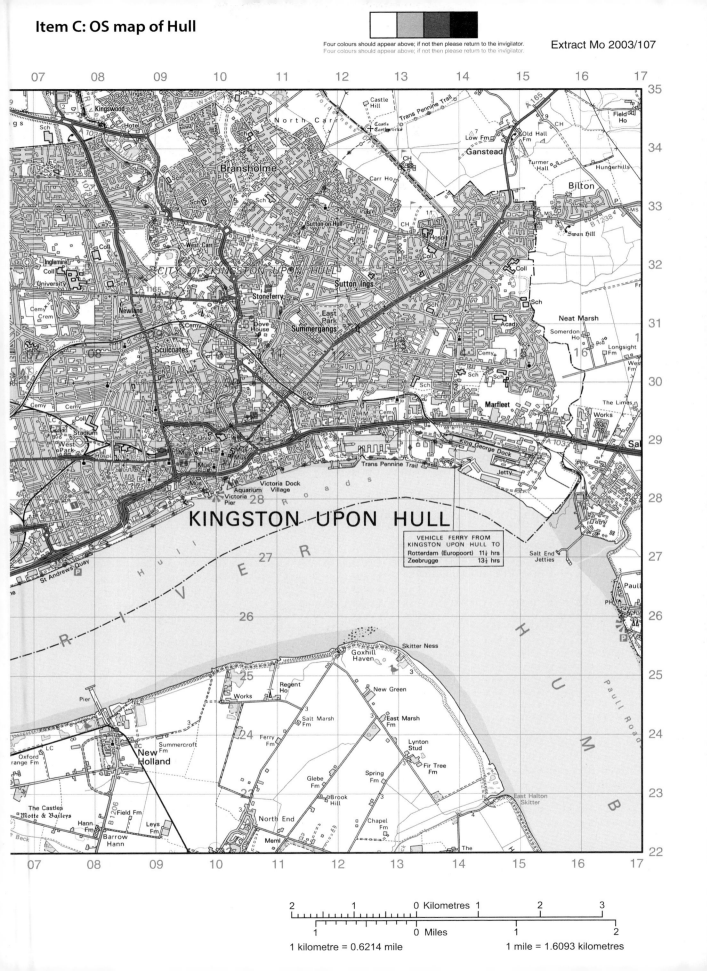

Item C: OS map of Hull

Four colours should appear above; if not then please return to the invigilator.
Four colours should appear above; if not then please return to the invigilator.

Extract Mo 2003/107

KINGSTON UPON HULL

| VEHICLE FERRY FROM |
| KINGSTON UPON HULL TO |

| Rotterdam (Europoort) | 11½ hrs |
| Zeebrugge | 13½ hrs |

1 kilometre = 0.6214 mile

1 mile = 1.6093 kilometres

EXAM C

Total marks — 60

Duration — 1 hour and 30 minutes

SECTION 1 — PHYSICAL ENVIRONMENTS — 20 marks

In this section you must answer: **EITHER** Question 1 **OR** Question 2, **AND** Questions 3, 4 and 5.

SECTION 2 — HUMAN ENVIRONMENTS — 20 marks

In this section you must answer Questions 6, 7 and 8.

SECTION 3 — GLOBAL ISSUES — 20 marks

Attempt any **TWO** questions

Question   9 — Climate Change

Question 10 — Impact of Human Activity on the Natural Environment

Question 11 — Environmental Hazards

Question 12 — Trade and Globalisation

Question 13 — Tourism

Question 14 — Health

SECTION 1 — PHYSICAL ENVIRONMENTS

In this section you must answer **EITHER** Question 1 **OR** Question 2, **AND** Questions 3, 4 and 5

Question 1: Glaciated Uplands

See Item A: OS map of Arran

a) Study the OS map **Item A** of the Arran area, extract number 2005/69.
    Match the glaciated uplands features shown below with the correct grid reference.
    pyramidal peak, arête, corrie
    992416, 998438, 995409, 981401   **3**

b) **Explain** the formation of an arête.
    You may use a diagram(s) in your answer.   **4**

Total marks 7

NOW ANSWER QUESTIONS 3, 4 AND 5

DO NOT ANSWER THIS QUESTION IF YOU HAVE ALREADY ANSWERED QUESTION 1

Question 2: Upland Limestone

See Item B: OS map of Malham

a) Study OS map **Item B** of the Malham area, extract number 1745/98

Use the information in the OS map **Item B** to match the features of upland limestone below with the correct grid reference.

pothole, limestone pavement, disappearing, stream

902647, 861681, 870660, 894657   **3**

b) **Explain** the formation of a limestone pavement.

You may use a diagram(s) in your answer.   **4**

Total marks   7

NOW ANSWER QUESTIONS 3, 4 AND 5

NOW ANSWER QUESTIONS 3, 4 and 5

Question 3

Study map extract Item A of the Arran area

Explain ways in which the physical landscape has affected land use on the map extract.

5

Question 4

Diagram Q4: Synoptic Chart, 5 December 2013

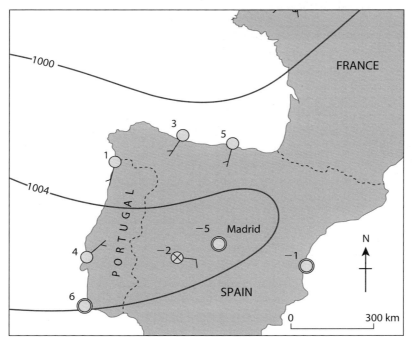

Study Diagram Q4.

Explain the weather conditions being experienced in Spain.

4

Question 5

Diagram Q5A: Landscape Types in the UK

| Glaciated Uplands | Upland Limestone | Coastal Landscapes | Rivers and Valleys |

Diagram Q5B: Land Uses in the UK

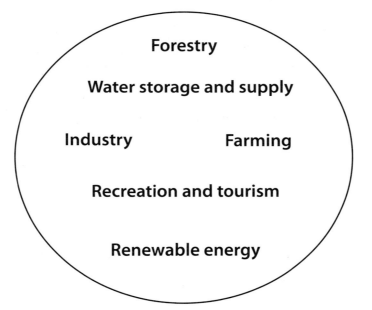

Forestry

Water storage and supply

Industry   Farming

Recreation and tourism

Renewable energy

Look at Diagrams Q5A and Q5B

Choose **one** landscape type you have studied from Diagram Q5A.

Select **two** land uses from Diagram Q5B.

Explain why your selected land uses are suitable for your chosen landscape type.   **4**

SECTION 2 — HUMAN ENVIRONMENTS

In this section you must answer Questions 6, 7 and 8

Question 6

See Item C: OS map of Kingston upon Hull

a) Study OS map **Item C** of the Kingston upon Hull area, extract number 2003/107

   Use map evidence to show that part of Kingston upon Hull's CBD is found in grid square 0928.   **3**

b) Using map evidence **describe, in detail**, the differences in the urban environments between grid square 0727 and grid square 0228.   **5**

Question 7

Diagram Q7: Development Indicators

Social Indicators	Economic Indicators
Life expectancy at birth	Gross domestic product (GDP)
Population per doctor	Energy used per person
Percentage adult literacy	Percentage population employed in agriculture

Study Diagram Q7.

Choose one social **and** one economic indicator.

Explain how your chosen indicators can show the level of development of a country.   **4**

Question 8

Diagram Q8: World Population Growth

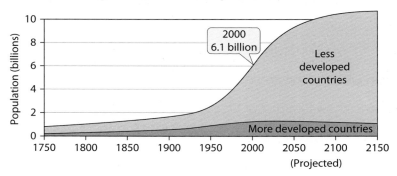

a) Look at Diagram Q8.

   Explain why the population of developing countries is growing far more rapidly than that of developed countries. **5**

b) **Describe** ways in which developing countries can reduce population growth. **3**

SECTION 3 — GLOBAL ISSUES

Answer any TWO questions

Question 9 — Climate Change

Question 10 — Impact of Human Activity on the Natural Environment

Question 11 — Environmental Hazards

Question 12 — Trade and Globalisation

Question 13 — Tourism

Question 14 — Health

Question 9: Climate Change

Diagram Q9A: Global Temperatures and Carbon Dioxide Emissions

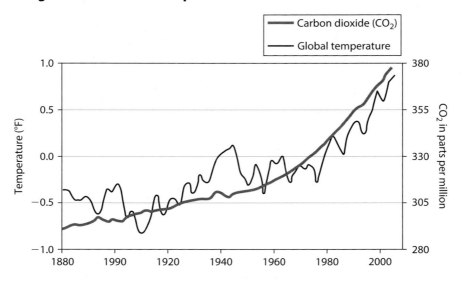

a) Study Diagram Q9A.

   Describe, **in detail**, the changes in global temperatures and carbon dioxide emissions.   **4**

Diagram Q9B: Some Solutions to Global Warming

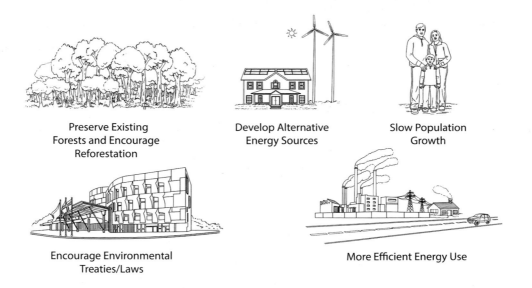

Preserve Existing Forests and Encourage Reforestation

Develop Alternative Energy Sources

Slow Population Growth

Encourage Environmental Treaties/Laws

More Efficient Energy Use

b) Look at Diagram Q9B.

   Choose **two** solutions from the diagram.

   Explain how each chosen solution could reduce global warming.   **6**

   Total marks   10

Question 10: Impact of Human Activity on the Natural Environment

Diagram Q10: Deforestation in Brazil, Bolivia and Peru

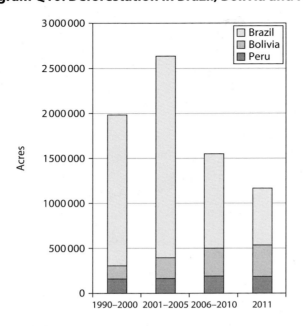

a) Study Diagram Q10.

    Describe, in detail, the changes in deforestation in Brazil, Bolivia and Peru.   **4**

b) **Explain** the benefits and problems of developing **either** the rainforest **or** the tundra.   **6**

Total marks 10

Question 11: Environmental Hazards

Diagram Q11A: Track of Selected July Tropical Storms

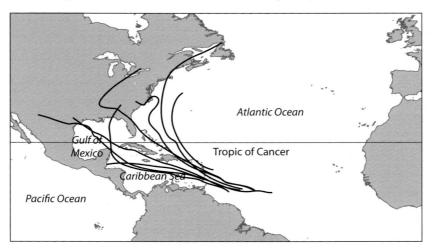

a)   Study Diagram Q11A.

Describe, in detail, the tracks of the tropical storms shown on Diagram Q11A.   **4**

Diagram Q11B: Areas Hit by Hurricane Katrina

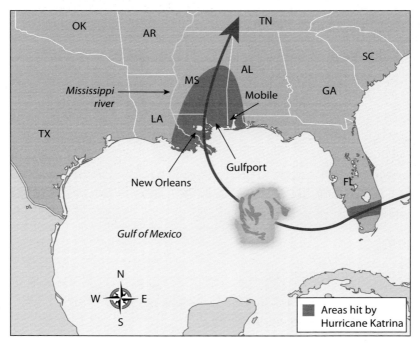

b)   Look at Diagram Q11B.

For a named hurricane, earthquake or volcanic eruption you have studied, **explain** the
impact on the people and environment of the area.   **6**

Total marks   10

Question 12: Trade and Globalisation

Diagram Q12A: UK's Export Trade with Selected Regions, 1999–2030 (projected)

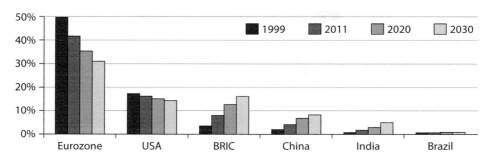

a) Study Diagram Q12A.

Describe, in detail, the projected changes in the UK's export trade between 1999 and 2030.   **4**

Diagram Q12B: Strategies to Protect Developing World Economies

b) Look at Diagram Q12B.

Choose either fair trade or cooperatives.

Explain how strategies like fair trade and cooperatives can protect the economy, people and environment of a developing world economy.   **6**

Total marks   10

Question 13: Tourism

Diagram Q13: Indian Tourism 1995–2012

Year	Tourist arrivals to India (millions)	India's share of world tourism (%)	Earnings from tourism (US $ billion)
1995	2.12	0.39	2.58
2000	2.65	0.39	3.46
2002	2.38	0.34	2.92
2004	3.46	0.45	6.17
2006	4.45	0.53	8.63
2008	5.28	0.57	11.75
2010	5.58	1.12	14.19
2012	6.66	1.29	15.95

a) Study Diagram Q13.

Describe, in detail, the trends in Indian tourism between 1995 and 2012. **4**

b) For any named country you have studied, **give ways** in which the effects of tourism can be controlled and managed. **6**

Total marks 10

Question 14: Health

Diagram Q14: Heart Attacks in Scotland and England (2002–2010)

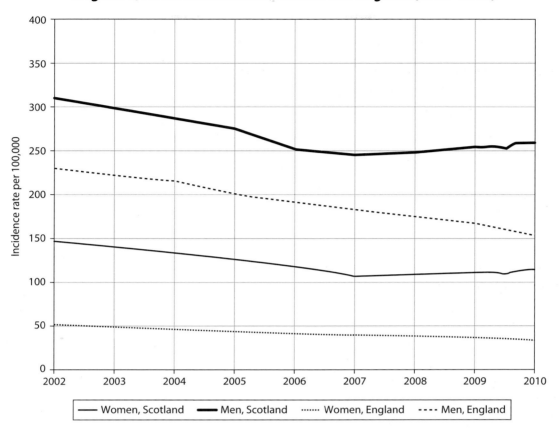

a) Study Diagram Q14.

   Describe, in detail, the differences in numbers of heart attacks between Scotland and England. **4**

b) For **either** malaria, cholera, heart disease **or** cancer **explain** the main causes of the disease and describe some methods used to combat the disease. **6**

Total marks 10

[END OF QUESTION PAPER]

How your paper will be marked

In this section you have the opportunity to see how questions are marked by the marker.

One question has been taken from each of the practice papers in this book and two sample answers for each have been provided. Explanations of the marks achieved have been provided to help you identify the differences between a poor/good/excellent answer

A marker needs to follow marking instructions and takes the following into account:

- Knowledge of the subject – has the candidate answered the question?

- If a question asks for explanation then the marker will allocate marks to statements that give reasons but not to simple descriptions (see types of question on page 7).

- If a question asks for two different points to be discussed then for the marker to allocate full marks both points must be mentioned. For example, if a question is marked out of six and asks for human and physical factors then both need to be mentioned for full marks. Marks are not necessarily allocated 3:3. For example, four marks could be allocated to one factor and two to the other, or five marks to one factor and one mark to the other. This allocation varies according to the marking instructions given to markers.

- If the question asks for differences then that needs to be made clear to the marker in the answer, e.g. "it is cloudy in Scotland **whereas** it's sunny in England".

- If map evidence is asked for then the marker is looking for reference to the specific map being used.

- In 'skills' questions, basic facts should be given based on the graph/diagram used. Quote dates, directions, figures or trends.

- Information lifted straight from a diagram will achieve very few marks, if any. The information needs to be processed/explained in some way.

Exam A, Question 14b (Global Issues)

For a disease you have studied, **explain** the consequences of the disease for the population in an affected area.

You should refer to examples you have studied in your answer. **6**

Answer 1

Malaria is common in poor countries like Nigeria. The disease is caused by a mosquito biting a human. This causes the person to become ill and unable to work (✓). If the person takes lots of time off then they may lose their job (✓). In many poor countries, farming is the main industry and problems will be caused if a person cannot go to work (✓). People are sometimes forced to move away from their village to escape breeding mosquitoes (✓). Many babies will be affected as there is a lack of mosquito nets and health care (✓). If the mosquito is not killed the disease will keep on spreading.

Comments/Marking

In general, one valid point will gain you a mark. If an answer is worth 6 marks you need to make six points.

This is a good answer but with room for improvement. On the whole it makes relevant points on the effects on the people. However, the first two sentences and the last sentence are not effects but simple descriptions of where the disease occurs and information about the mosquito. These are not relevant to this question so gain no marks. The next sentences are appropriate explanations so gain marks. The statement on people not being able to work on farms is a repeat (R) of the previous point so gains no marks. Remember, the question asks for explanation so your answer should show how the people are affected. This answer would get 4 out 6 marks.

Answer 2

Nigeria is a country I have studied where 97% of the population is at risk from malaria. A consequence for people living in areas affected is that sufferers can no longer work (✓), not only that but other people also spend time looking after them which further decreases the workforce (✓). If too much time is taken off work then they may lose their job (✓), reducing the family income making it difficult to feed their families (✓) and causing an increase in poverty in general (✓), as well as decreasing the economy of the area (✓). Malaria is a major public health problem in Nigeria where it accounts for more cases and deaths than any other country in the world (✓). If not seen by a doctor, a person infected with malaria has a risk of not surviving (✓). Medicines and treatment are expensive but not being able to work means that the person finds it difficult to pay for medicines and treatment (✓) thus increasing the burden on their families (✓). People are sometimes forced to leave their homes and fields to get away from malaria infected areas and this can result in hardship as they lose their homes and their livelihood (✓).

Comments/Marking

This is an excellent answer which correctly identifies the consequences of living with malaria. It begins well by referring to an appropriate named area, Nigeria, and includes facts on Nigeria in the answer. This shows your depth of knowledge of a particular area to the marker. The question asks for a case study you have studied so, by inserting appropriate facts, this answer can achieve full marks. This answer would get full marks, 6 out of 6. In fact, sufficient points were made to gain 11 marks!

Exam B, Question 3 (Physical Environments)

Diagram Q3: The Mawddach Way, Barmouth

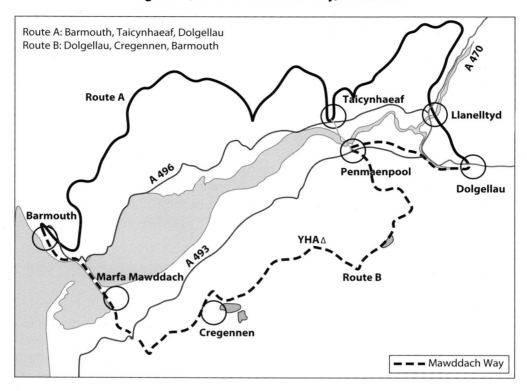

Route A: Barmouth, Taicynhaeaf, Dolgellau
Route B: Dolgellau, Cregennen, Barmouth

Study Diagram Q3 and OS map Item A of the Barmouth area.

A group of walkers have the choice of walking Route A or Route B of the Mawddach Way.

For either Route A or Route B, **describe the advantages and disadvantages** of the route. You must use map evidence in your answer.

5

Answer 1

I think they should choose Route A. It has plenty of parking at the start. It is close to the National Park with mountains and forests. There is a nature reserve at 687194 (✓) where a variety of wildlife can be seen (✓). There is a hotel where you could get a drink and food (✓). It is away from towns so will be a peaceful walk (✓) but there is a telephone box at 691194 where they could contact the police if there was an emergency (✓). The route could be difficult for children as it is quite high in places (✓) and it passes an old mine.

Comments/Marking

This is a good answer but takes a while to get to the point. The first three statements are descriptions. To gain marks, an advantage or disadvantage of the feature identified needs to be given, e.g. the forests can be used for picnicking or bird spotting. One mark is gained for giving an appropriate grid reference at 687194. Another correct grid reference is given for the telephone box but the mark has already been given for the nature reserve. The answer also concentrates more on the advantages of the walk, with only one mark being gained for the disadvantages. Passing an old mine needs to be expanded to include the point that it spoils the view. This answer would achieve full marks, 5 out of 5, four marks coming from the advantages and one mark from the disadvantages. If no disadvantages had been given this answer would achieve 4 marks.

Answer 2

My choice is Route B

The advantages of this route are that there is a variety of scenery along the walk (✓), from views of the coast, to mountains and rivers (✓). A variety of wildlife can be seen in these areas (✓), from sea birds on the coast to deer on the mountains (✓). There are places along the route to stop for something to eat such as the picnic site (✓) at 697153 (✓). There are no settlements in the area so there will be limited traffic, meaning the route will be quiet and peaceful (✓).

The disadvantages of the route are that it is quite high up so could be a difficult climb for small children (✓) and it could be dangerous going down as it is quite steep (✓) at 658145 (✓), At 240 metres it could be cold (✓) so walkers would need to carry warm clothing. There are very few places to stop along the route so getting something to eat and drink would be difficult (✓) and they would need to carry it with them making their packs heavy (✓).

Comment/Marking

This is a better answer. It is well organised. It separates the advantages from the disadvantages making it clearer for the marker. It uses map evidence to support each statement and gives an appropriate grid reference which gains one mark. As requested it gives a balance of advantages and disadvantages. Unlike the first answer it takes each statement made and backs it up with evidence from the map. There are seven marks available for the advantages and six marks for the disadvantages so easily gains full marks, 5 out of 5.

Exam C, Question 7 (Human Environments)

Diagram Q7: Development Indicators

Social Indicators	Economic Indicators
Life expectancy at birth	Gross domestic product (GDP)
Population per doctor	Energy used per person
Percentage adult literacy	Percentage population employed in agriculture

Study Diagram Q7.

Choose one social **and** one economic indicator.

Explain how your chosen indicators can show the level of development of a country.   **4**

Answer 1

I have chosen Population per doctor. This means the number of people in an area allocated to one doctor. In some areas of the world there are large numbers of people to one doctor while in others there are less people to one doctor. It is better to have a small number of people to one doctor.

My second indicator is Percentage population employed in agriculture. This is the number of people who work in farming. Farming is a primary industry and more people are employed in poor countries as they don't have many other jobs in industry (✓).

Comment/Answer

This is a poor answer. It does not answer the question. It is a description of the indicator not how that indicator can be used to tell about the development of a country. There is one mark at the end, although it's not too specific, as it implies there are few people employed in industry where more money is made so a country doesn't have money to develop. In this case the pupil made the correct choice of one economic and one social indicator. If the answer was related to only one type of indicator then only two marks would be available. This answer achieves only 1 out of 4.

Answer 2

The social indicator I have chosen is Population per doctor. This is the number of the people to one doctor. The lower the number of people per doctor the better, because countries with a low population per doctor are normally more developed which means they have a better health care system (✓) with more doctors trained meaning less patients per doctor (✓). This means that the country is also wealthy enough to be able to afford to invest money in a health care system (✓).

The economic indicator I have chosen is Percentage population employed in agriculture. A low percentage employed in agriculture usually shows a more developed country which means more people are employed in industry (✓). This means that people have a higher standard of living (✓) as these jobs pay better than jobs in farming (✓).

Comment/Marking

This is a very good answer. Two appropriate indicators have been discussed. The indicator has not just been described (which would in this case achieve no marks) but used to explain how it shows development. It makes three good points about each indicator achieving a possible six points for a four point answer. This answer achieves 4 out of 4.

Have a go yourself!

Marking is a good way to improve your exam technique and knowledge of the course. Mark your own answers to the practice papers following the hints and guidelines in this book. This will show you if your answers are too short, if they don't have enough detail in them, or don't answer the question. If you have a study partner you could mark each other's papers! You can then discuss/justify your marking. This will give you a better understanding of the questions and what is expected in an answer.

After you have completed the practice papers, have a go at marking the following answers (there are no marking schemes for these three questions). Mark the questions and then compare your marking with a study partner. Be prepared to explain why you did or did not give marks for a particular point!

Question 1

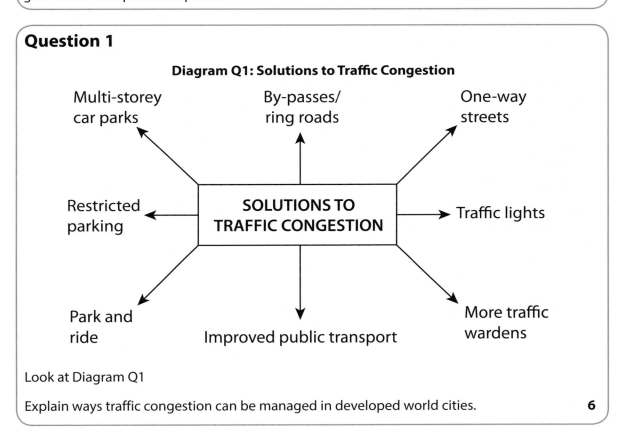

Diagram Q1: Solutions to Traffic Congestion

Look at Diagram Q1

Explain ways traffic congestion can be managed in developed world cities.   **6**

Answer

If you improve public transport more people will use buses, train, etc., and fewer people will use cars so the roads will become less congested. If fewer people use their cars it will also cause greenhouse gases to decrease. In addition, the transport company will make a profit – lots more people will use their services. However, buses and trains can be expensive so more people will use their cars rather than pay high prices. Also if the bus breaks down there will be more people let down and they may start to use their own cars again. Bypasses and ring roads allow traffic to go round the city instead of through which reduces the amount of cars in the city centre. Park and Ride schemes allow cars to be parked outside the city and a train can then be taken into the city. Trains carry more passengers thus reducing the cars entering the city.

Question 2

Diagram Q2: Birth rate for the UK and Chad

Country	Birth rate per 1000 of the population
United Kingdom	12
Chad	39

Look at Diagram Q2.

Give reasons to explain the differences in birth rates between a developed country such as the UK and a developing country such as Chad.   **4**

Answer

Reasons for the difference in birth rates between a developed country and a developing country are as follows. In developing countries, people depend on their children to help bring in money for their families and in olden days a lot of children used to die because they didn't have proper health care services. Families still think that their children will die so have a lot to make up for the ones they think they will lose. However, in a developed country, we don't depend on our children to help bring in money for the family and we know the chance of our children dying is less likely so our birth rate is lower. Developed countries that have more medical care have fewer children as there is more chance of them surviving.

Question 3

For a named natural disaster you have studied, explain methods use to reduce/manage the effects of a disaster.   **6**

Answer

In a hurricane, people are given warnings on the television days before it arrives to give them time to leave their homes and go to shelter somewhere safer. People can board up their houses and businesses to reduce damage. Some buildings are fitted with hurricane shutters to protect the property. Routes to take are signposted so that areas can be evacuated quickly. People get leaflets explaining what to do in a hurricane. People are warned of the danger of staying in their homes if they have been told to leave.

Answers to Practice Exams

Exam A Marking Scheme

Question 1

a) Headland = 795804

  Bay = 807803

  Stack = 834796   **3**

b) A headland is an area of land which juts out into the sea (1) and is surrounded by the sea on three sides (1). Headlands form along coastlines where the land meets the sea at 90 degrees (1) and where there are layers of hard and soft rock (1). The coastline is eroded by the processes of hydraulic action (1), i.e. the force of the water hitting the cliffs (1), corrasion (1), i.e. where waves pick up stones and toss them at the cliffs (1), and corrosion (1), i.e. where the rocks are dissolved by sea water (1). The harder, more resistant chalks erode more slowly to form headlands whereas softer rocks erode faster to form bays (2).

**Below is an example of a sketch you could include in your answer;
a fully labelled diagram could get you full marks.**

The Formation of Headlands and Bays

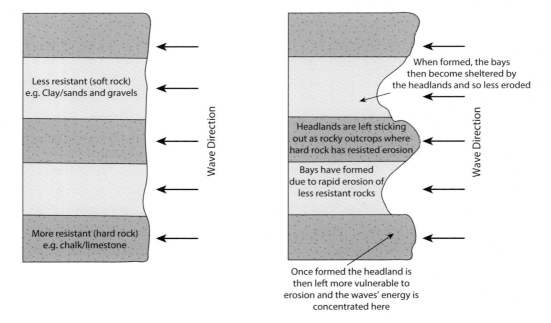

                                                                                                        4

> **HINT**   Avoid simply describing the feature. You must explain the processes involved. Also mention in your answer examples of the coastline you have studied, e.g. Jurassic Coast.

A sample answer for the formation of caves, arches and stacks:

Waves widen weaknesses or cracks in the rock (1), mainly by the process of hydraulic action (1). The cracks gradually get larger and develop into small caves (1). Erosion further widens the cave (1) and the roof of the arch is weathered by frost, wind and rain (1). The structure becomes weakened and eventually the roof of the arch collapses inwards leaving a stack (1). The stack is attacked at the base (1). This weakens the structure and it will eventually collapse to form a stump (1).

Below is an example of a sketch you could include in your answer; a fully labelled diagram could get you full marks.

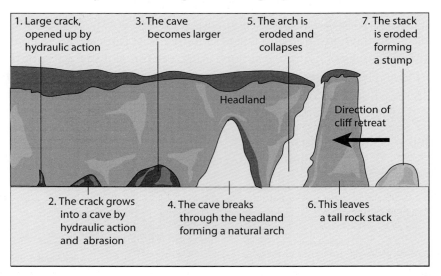

4

Question 2

a) River flowing southeast = 813890

Meander = 805880

Ox-bow lake = 839875   3

b) In the upper course of a river water flows quickly through a narrow channel with a steep gradient (1). It uses this energy to deepen its bed (1) this is called vertical erosion (1). The river carries stones and rocks in the water, and the force of the water and the grinding of rocks and stones cut down into the river bed by abrasion (2). Rocks on the valley sides can be broken down by freeze-thaw or chemical weathering (1) and mass movements carry this loose material down the valley and into the river (1). The river transports this material downstream (1).

**Below is an example of a sketch you could include in your answer;
a fully labelled diagram could get you full marks.**

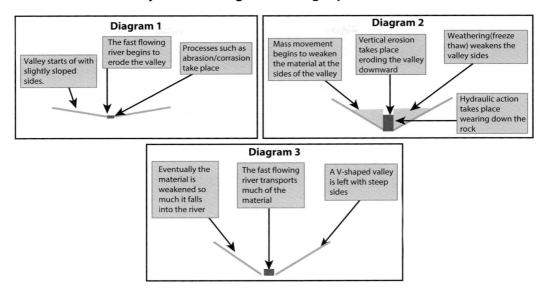

4

HINT

You should try to use a diagram to support your answer. A well-drawn and labelled diagram could achieve full marks. You should mention the processes involved in the formation.

A sample answer for the formation of an ox bow lake:

A river meanders across a valley (1). It erodes from side to side (1), flows fastest on the outside of the bend, causing more erosion there (1), and flows more slowly on the inside of the bend so material is deposited there (1). The erosion narrows the neck of the meander (1) and during a flood the river will flow straight through the neck (1) forming a new course (1). Eventually the meander is cut off (1), new deposition seals off the ends, and the cut-off becomes an ox-bow lake (1).

Below is an example of a sketch you could include in your answer; a fully labelled diagram could get you full marks.

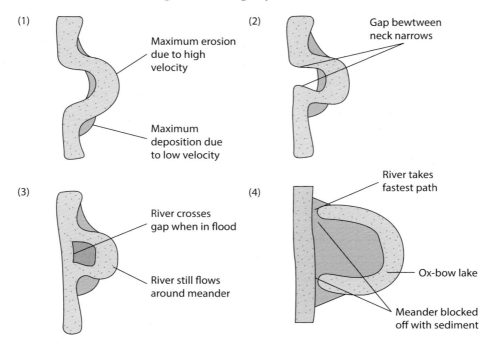

4

Question 3

A = A352

B = Railway

C = River Frome

D = Tank training area

E = Coniferous wood

4

Question 4

> **HINT** When answering this type of question you can give both sides of the argument to support your answer. Remember not to simply describe the weather, you need to use the information on the weather chart to support your choice. You can choose either Chart A or Chart B.

If Chart A chosen:

There is a cold front over southern Ireland, northern Wales and central England which brings heavy rain and this is the weather shown on Diagram Q4A (1). Cold fronts bring cloudy weather and this is indicated on Diagram Q4A (1). The chart shows that the isobars are closer together in western Scotland and northern Ireland, and this is reflected by the higher wind speeds of 35mph in these areas as opposed to 10mph in southern England (1). There is high pressure approaching from the south explaining the higher temperatures there (1). Chart B shows a warm front in eastern England which brings rain but Diagram Q4A shows sunny dry weather (1) with light cloud cover (1).

If Chart B chosen:

There is a cold front over southern Ireland, northern Wales and central England which brings heavy rain and this is the weather shown on Diagram Q4A (1). Cold fronts bring cloudy weather and this is indicated on Diagram Q4A (1). The south of the UK is in the warm sector of a depression so it is warmer and drier as is shown on Diagram Q4A (1). Winds are light in southwest England due to the approaching high pressure (1).   **4**

Question 5

HINT Make sure you describe a conflict between two land uses, do not simply list general conflicts. Refer to the specific landscape type you have studied and give examples of the conflict. For full marks you need to mention both conflict and solution.

If Glaciated Uplands chosen:

Recreation and Tourism/Farming:

Walkers with dogs may worry sheep (1). Tourists leave gates open allowing animals to escape (1) and drop litter which animals may eat (1). Farmers may restrict access (1). Tourists could park over field access gates blocking the farmer's access to his fields (1). Traffic congestion caused by slow moving tractors (1). Unpleasant smells from spreading slurry (1).

Solutions:

Number of car parks has been increased to take traffic off narrow country roads and to prevent inconsiderate parking (2). Educate the public about the Countryside Code (1). Bodies such as the National Parks Authority distribute leaflets, have slide shows and video presentations, and have well informed Information Assistants to talk to the visitors (2). Information panels at important sites and car parks, giving specific details about a site and advice on access (2). Construction of ladder stiles over walls and step stiles through fences where rights of way cross these field boundaries (2). Sign all public footpaths and post specific notices during lambing and haymaking to ask visitors to be especially considerate of farmers' needs (2).   **5**

Question 6

HINT You must give both advantages and disadvantages for full marks. You need to give reasons for each point, e.g. don't just say flat land, say why the flat land is good, i.e. for building on. Give examples from the map.

a) **Advantages:**

The land is flat for building on (1), there is plenty of land for expansion (1) and a large flat area for parking (1). Wool is nearby so people will come from there to shop (1), and people living there could work at the shopping centre (1).

Disadvantages:

A river runs through the square reducing the available building land (1); the river could flood, damaging the buildings and contents (1). There are no main roads into the area so transporting goods in and out would be difficult (1) and access for customers would also be difficult (1).   **5**

b) There has been a very small drop in spending on crop chemicals (1). The largest increase in spending has been on GM crops (1) which has more than doubled to £2.4 billion (1). The spending on fertilizers has increased only slightly (1). The spending on farm machinery has increased greatly (1) from £0.75 billion to £1.6 billion (1). Spending on animal genetics has increased slightly (1).   **3**

> *HINT*   Marks can be gained by quoting actual figures from the graph and also by processing them.

Question 7

> *HINT*   The question asks for an explanation so you must give reasons. You may get a maximum of 2 marks for only describing the changes.

In stage 3, the death rate continues to fall due to continued improvements in medicine (1) and increased standards of living (1). The birth rate falls rapidly with the growth of family planning (1) and smaller families are needed as fewer babies die (1). Population grows rapidly at the beginning of stage 3 due to the differences in the birth and death rates (1), but growth levels off at the end of stage 3 as the birth rate and death rate reach similar low levels (1).

In stage 4, a decreasing birth rate is shown with people wanting smaller (cheaper) families (1), women following careers, greater access to family planning (contraception/abortion) (2), a decreasing death rate and increasing life expectancy due to improved health care, sanitation, housing, food supply (2), pensions and care for the elderly (1). Low birth rates and low death rates mean very low population growth (1).   **6**

Question 8

If Large number of pedestrians chosen:

Many people work in the city and so travel into the city to their employment (1) in the large number of offices, department stores and shops (1). This results in there being many pedestrians, especially at morning and evening rush hours (1). Many people are attracted to the undercover shopping centres (1) like the Buchanan Galleries in Glasgow (1). There are many public/government buildings like the Town Hall which attract many people on a daily basis (1). The city centre is a tourist attraction so visitors come into the city to visit the museums and historical buildings (1). The city centre has many restaurants, clubs and pubs attracting large numbers of people every day (1).

> *HINT*   Try to give named examples from a city you know. Remember to give reasons for the features, not a description.

If Tall/high density buildings chosen:

Land values tend to be very high (1) due to lack of space and competition for land (1). Buildings tend to be multi-storey due to the high land values resulting in building up rather than out (1). Many buildings are multi-purpose, e.g. shops, offices and restaurants in the same building, as there is limited open space available (1).

If Congestion and pollution chosen:

Many British cities still have street plans that were laid down hundreds of years ago so the roads are narrow and not designed for cars (2). The roads cannot cope with the ever-increasing numbers of cars and other vehicles causing massive congestion problems, especially at rush hour (2). There are more cars on the road due to an increase in disposable income (1). There are less people using public transport (1) and an increase in commuting (for work, shopping, and entertainment) (1). Air pollution is caused by the many vehicles crowding into the city every day (1), especially by vehicles stuck in traffic jams (1); frustrated drivers using their horns causes noise pollution (1).

If Department Stores and hotels chosen:

Department stores are located in the CBD because they require a large threshold population (1). Large numbers of people come to this area as this is the most accessible part of the city (1) – most of the transport routes lead here (1) as the main bus and train stations are located here (1). Land values are high and large stores can afford to locate here (1). Hotels are located here because many tourists are attracted to the sites and facilities of the CBD and so will use the facilities offered by hotels (1).

Each of these answers would not be worth 6 marks.

The whole question, which asks for two features, is out of 6.

> *HINT* Remember that you only need to answer two Global Issues questions. Knowing the location of some countries of the world will be useful in the Global Issues section.

Question 9

> *HINT* When answering part (a), remember the answers are on the diagram. Try to give as much detail as you can. To gain marks you need to name actual countries or areas. This answer is purely description – no explanation is required and marks will not be awarded for explanation.

a) Countries like Australia, New Zealand and Indonesia have the lowest risk (1). Most of western Europe and northern Europe is at greatest risk (1). Examples of countries most at risk are Russia, China, India and South Africa (1). The countries of North Africa with a Mediterranean coastline are also at most risk (1). The USA and Canada have a moderate risk (1). **4**

b) **Physical causes may include:**

Changes in solar activity can increase or decrease temperatures (1), e.g. a decrease in solar activity is thought to have triggered the Little Ice Age between 1650 and 1850 (1). Gases and dust particles released during volcanic eruptions block the sun's rays leading to a cooling of the earth (1), e.g. in 1991 the eruption of Mount Pinatubo released 17 million tonnes of sulphur dioxide which reduced global sunlight by 10% (1) cooling the planet by 0.5°C for a year (1). The greenhouse gas methane, is naturally released from arctic tundra and wetlands (1). This traps heat in the earth's atmosphere causing temperatures to rise (1). Changes in the earth's orbit can affect the severity of the seasons (1) – more tilt means warmer summers and colder winters, while less tilt means cooler summers and milder winters (1).

> **HINT** The question asks for an explanation so you must give reasons in your answer.

Human causes may include:

The production of electricity from fossil fuels is responsible for the emission of huge amounts of greenhouse gases and other pollutants which trap gases in the atmosphere (2). Cars, buses and trucks run mainly on petrol or diesel, both are fossil fuels which create greenhouse gases (1). People produce large quantities of waste such as plastics which remain in the environment for many years and release gases which contribute to greenhouse gases (2). Timber is used in great quantities for construction of houses; large areas of forest have to be cut down and so there are fewer trees to absorb the carbon dioxide which is trapped in the atmosphere (2). Increasing populations mean more food is needed and so more fertilizers are used, increasing the amount of nitrous oxide in the atmosphere (2). **6**

> **HINT** You must refer to both human and physical factors in your answer.

Question 10

> **HINT** Using figures in your answer will increase your marks.

a) Oil production decreased between 1981 and 2011 (1) from 550 million barrels to 200 million barrels (1). Production rose between 1981 and 1989 (1) by 160 billion barrels (1). The highest production was in 1988 at around 710 million barrels (1). Production has fallen steadily between 1989 and 2011 (1). **4**

b) In the Prudhoe Bay area of Alaska oil drilling and the construction of the Trans-Alaskan pipeline has caused damage to the tundra vegetation and wildlife (1). In places, the pipeline stops the caribou migrating (1). Local Inuit people have had their way of life disrupted as they have to make long detours around the pipeline and therefore no longer have access to some of their traditional hunting grounds (1). The traditional way of life of the Inuit is being destroyed as the younger generation comes into contact with Western ways and they leave for the big cities, or turn to drink and drugs (2). The Inuit were promised jobs in the oil industry but there are very few jobs available and are poorly paid (1). The oil industry has brought great wealth to the people of Alaska who have the highest average income in the USA (2). In coastal areas of Greenland climate change is adversely affecting the habitat of animals such as the polar bear (1). The hunting traditions of the Inuit are disrupted as the sea is frozen for a shorter time – people and polar bears are not able to hunt for as much of the year (2). **6**

Question 11

> **HINT** Try to use named areas when describing distribution. Try to give examples you have studied in your answer.

a) The main concentration of these earthquakes is around the Pacific Ring of Fire (1). There is a large concentration around the Indonesian islands (1). There are also a lot along the west coast of North and South America (1), but with a higher concentration in South America (1). There are some located in the north of India and the Himalayas (1), and some located around the eastern Mediterranean (1). There are very few in Africa (1) and none inland or on the east coast of North and South America (2). **4**

b) **If an Earthquake is chosen:**

Earthquake resistant buildings are built with deep foundations, rubber shock absorbers and concrete reinforced with steel (1). They are designed to twist and sway instead of collapsing (1). They have sprinkler systems and gas cut-off valves to prevent fire spreading (1). People living in areas prone to earthquakes, such as San Francisco, have emergency plans in place (1) and supplies such as bottled water, medicines, tinned food etc., are stockpiled by individuals or the local area to ensure they have vital supplies in an emergency (1). Earthquake drills are held in order to practise what to do in the event of an earthquake (1). Warning systems are put in place to give enough time to allow people to move to a safer location (1). **6**

If a Volcano is chosen:

Technological advances are making it easier to predict volcanic eruptions giving people enough warning to evacuate an area before an eruption (1). Exclusion zones are put around the area so fewer people should be killed or injured if an eruption occurs (1), e.g. Mount St. Helens (1). Satellites monitor the temperature and shape of active volcanoes (1). Sensors measure levels of sulphur dioxide and carbon dioxide gas which can give advanced warning of volcanic eruptions (1). Seismometers record earthquakes as magma rises to fill the volcano (1). Tilt meters record any change in the shape of the volcano giving early warning of an eruption (1). **6**

Question 12

a) China's economy is predicted to grow by around $7trillion by 2020 (1). It has also moved from 7th in the world up to 2nd (1). Japan is predicted to move down from 2nd in the world to 3rd (1). Germany is also predicted to fall from 3rd to 4th (1). India's economy is growing and is predicted to move from being the 12th largest in the world to 9th (1). **4**

> **HINT** Use figures in the diagrams to put detail into your answer. Answers must refer to changes.

b) More money goes directly to the farmer, it cuts out the middlemen who take some of the profits (1). Farmers receive a guaranteed minimum price so they are not affected as much by price fluctuations (1) and can receive some money in advance so they don't run short (1). More of the money goes to the communities who can invest it in improving their living conditions (1). Money can be used to provide electricity and drinking water, and to pay for education (1). Fair trade also encourages farmers to treat their workers well (1) and to look after the environment (1). **6**

Question 13

a) The greatest increase in tourist arrivals is in southeast Asia (1), up by 10% (1). Tourist arrivals in areas like South America, central eastern Europe and India have increased by around 8% (1). Sub-Saharan Africa, the UK and Scandinavia have seen numbers increase by about 5% (1). Tourist arrivals in other places such as North America and northeast Asia are increasing but much more slowly (1). Numbers for Australia are growing more slowly, by about 1% (1), while tourist arrivals to North Africa and the Middle East have decreased (1) by around 10% (1). **4**

b) Advantages: Tourism brings money into the area and has made Benidorm one of the most prosperous areas in Spain (1). New jobs are created in hotels, restaurants and attractions, reducing the unemployment levels (1) as well as reducing the number of young people who leave looking for jobs in the city (1). The increased money from tourism has been used to improve the infrastructure, such as new roads to Alicante airport (1). The facilities created for use by the tourists can also improve the social life of the locals (1). Farmers make more money as there is an increased demand for their produce (1), or they may sell some of their farmland to make way for new hotels etc. (1).

Disadvantages: However, many hotels were needed to meet the demand. They were built quickly and are of poor quality as there was little planning control (2). High-rise buildings were built to accommodate as many tourists as possible, detracting from the scenery (1). There was a loss of farmland resulting in a loss of jobs (1). There was a loss of culture and the traditional way of life as British food was imported to satisfy the tourists (1). **6**

> **HINT** Remember to give reasons as the question asks for explanation.

Question 14

a) The number of infectious diseases is predicted to decrease between 2002 and 2030 in both high-income and low-income countries, and therefore also across the world as a whole (2). It is predicted that the number of infectious diseases will fall across the world by 11%, from 41% in 2002 to 30% in 2030 (1). In high-income countries it is predicted that the number of infectious diseases will fall from 6% in 2002 to 3% in 2030 (1), while in low-income countries the number will decrease from 56% in 2002 to 41% in 2030 (1).

The number of non-infectious diseases are predicted to increase between 2002 and 2030 in both high-income and low-income countries, and therefore also across the world as a whole (2). It is predicted that the number of non-infectious diseases will rise across the world by 10%, from 47% in 2002 to 57% in 2030 (1). In high-income countries it is predicted that the number of non-infectious diseases will rise from 85% in 2002 to 90% in 2030 (1), while in low-income countries the number will increase from 33% in 2002 to 45% in 2030 (1). **4**

> **HINT** Try to give general trends as well as giving specific figures.

b) **If Malaria is chosen:**

Malaria is the second biggest cause of death from infectious disease in African countries such as Nigeria and Uganda (1). The people who survive malaria become very weak through illness (1) and, as medical care can be expensive, the burden of care for the sick usually falls on family members (1). When a person becomes ill with malaria they often cannot work (1) and are therefore unable to earn money (1). With little or no money coming in families may suffer as they cannot afford essentials such as food, shelter or education for the young (2). As more people contract malaria and become unable to work the earning power of the affected area is reduced (1). As a result, the government may divert investment away from other services, such as education, to the maintenance of health care facilities and the purchasing of drugs for treating malaria (2). **6**

You can find more detailed markers' comments for this question in the 'How your paper will be marked' section.

HINT If asked for an area you have studied try to insert some specific facts into your answer. On some occasions, one mark might be deducted for not mentioning a specific area/case study in your answer.

If Heart disease is chosen:

Many work days are lost in industry through ill health (1), which can reduce profits in business (1). Strain is put on the health service, increasing the cost of state and private healthcare (1) as more medical staff and hospital beds are needed to treat those suffering from the disease (1). There is an increase in the number of patients suffering from coronary-related illnesses such as angina, high blood pressure and strokes (1). Life expectancy is lowered (1). **6**

If AIDS is chosen:

If young people are infected with HIV/AIDS they might die leading to a shortage of labour in some areas and countries (1). Lack of staff in schools means that children cannot be educated (1) and therefore cannot go on to get good jobs and find it difficult to support their families (1). If farmers or farm workers are ill they will be too weak to work meaning there might be food shortages (1) and people will not have enough food to survive (1). Industries will not have enough workers so the area/country cannot develop and might get into debt (1). The relatives of people suffering with HIV/AIDS may not be accepted by other members of their community and may lose their jobs and struggle to survive (1). Treating the sick in more remote areas can be difficult as some areas will not have access to qualified doctors, nurses and medicines (1). **6**

If Cholera is chosen:

Cholera can reduce the economic development of a country (1). Trade is affected as some countries restrict imports of certain foods if there is a cholera outbreak (1). Cholera can also negatively impact the tourism sector as countries stop or restrict travel from countries where a cholera outbreak is occurring, as well as advising people not to travel to that country (1); this can result in loss of livelihoods (1). Poor families may face hardship through paying for hospital stays and the medicine used to treat cholera (2). Countries face economic losses from the lost productivity of the carers (1). **6**

[END OF MARKING SCHEME]

Exam B Marking Scheme

Question 1

a) U-shaped valley = 723196

Corrie = 713141

Arête = 706115 **3**

b) **Plucking:** This occurs where ice freezes to the rock and pulls pieces away as it moves (1). This makes the back wall steeper (1) and provides tools for further erosion (1).

Abrasion: This occurs where rock fragments are used as tools to scrape the floor of the corrie (1), making it deeper/over-deepening it (1).

Frost shattering: This occurs when water enters cracks in the rocks, then freezes and expands (1). Repeated over and over, this levers fragments away from the rock (1), making the back wall steeper (1). The fragments become part of the glacier's load (1).

**Below is an example of a sketch you could include in your answer;
a fully labelled diagram could get you full marks.**

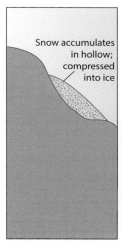

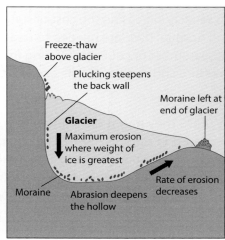

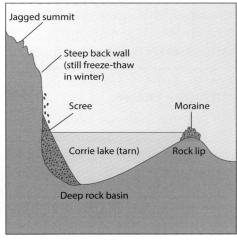

(a) Beginning of Ice Age   (b) During Ice Age   (c) After Ice Age

4

> **HINT** This question asks for processes. Your answer should concentrate on how the processes of freeze–thaw, plucking and abrasion form a corrie. You should use a diagram in your answer showing where these processes take place.

A sample answer for the formation of a U–shaped valley:

As the glacier moves down the valley (1) it deepens and widens the valley (1) by plucking and abrasion (1). The weight and erosive power of the ice remove the interlocking spurs (1). Rocks under the ice scrape soil and material from valley floor (1).

Below is an example of a sketch you could include in your answer; a fully labelled diagram could get you full marks.

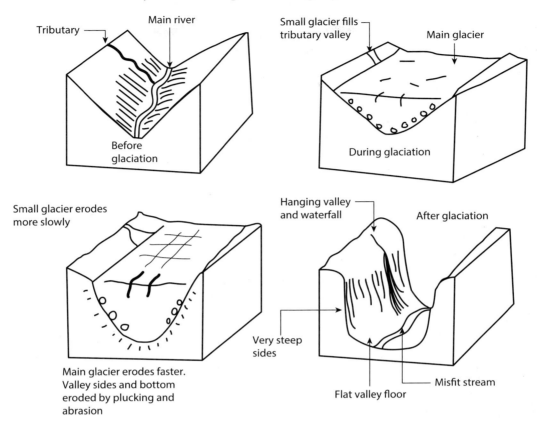

4

Question 2

a) V-shaped valley = 738150

River flowing southwest = 722200

Tributary = 671175   3

b) Waterfalls are found where hard rock, such as limestone, overlies softer rock, such as mudstone (1). The water is powerful and erodes the softer rock by hydraulic action (1) i.e. the sheer force of the water hitting off the rock (1). A plunge pool forms (1). The softer rock is worn away, the hard rock is undercut and an overhang of hard rock is left suspended above the plunge pool (2). This collapses as there is nothing to support it and the rock falls into the plunge pool (1). Rock fragments swirling around deepen the plunge pool (1). This process is repeated over a long period of time and the waterfall retreats upstream leaving a steep sided gorge (1).   4

> ***HINT***   Annotated diagrams will improve your answer and, if annotated properly, can gain full marks.

Question 3

If Route A chosen:

Advantages:

There is a train station where people can access the start of the walk (1) as well as parking areas (1). It passes through the National Park (1) with good views of the mountains (1). There is a forest for picnicking and bird watching (1), there is a hotel for food, and a comfort stop (1) at 675190 (1), there is a nature reserve at 687194 where a variety of wildlife can be seen (1). There is also a telephone box at 691194 from which emergency services could be contacted if needed (1). It does not pass through any settlements so should be peaceful (1).

Disadvantages:

Many areas along the route are quite high (1) at over 300m (1) which could be difficult for older walkers (1). There is a disused mine at 676201 (1) which could spoil the view (1). There are several rivers to be crossed, e.g. at 689200, which could be dangerous (1). There are only a few places along the route where they could buy food and drink (1).   **5**

> You can find more detailed markers' comments for this question in the 'How your paper will be marked' section.

> *HINT* For full marks you must mention both advantages and disadvantages. You will get one mark for an accurate grid reference.

If Route B chosen:

Advantages:

It passes through fine scenery (1) with good views of mountains at first, and later of the sea (1). There are varied habitats (moors, woodland, river and sea) for wildlife watching (2). There is a picnic site at 697153 (1) where they can stop for a snack (1). There is a telephone box at 698152 from which emergency services could be contacted if needed (2). It does not pass through any settlements so will be peaceful (1).

Disadvantages:

It climbs up to 240m (1) so might be difficult for older walkers (1). At this height it might be quite cold (1). The descent from 658145 is very steep, which could be dangerous (2). There are very few places on the route where they could buy food and drink (1).   **5**

Question 4

> *HINT* The marks for this question come from explanation, description will get you no marks. You need to compare the areas to get full marks. Try to use the words 'whereas' and 'because' in each of your points as this shows you are comparing the places and giving an explanation for the differences.

In the north of Scotland there is a cold front bringing cloudy conditions, whereas the south of England has no clouds because there is no front close by (1). The temperature in the north of Scotland is lower than in the south of England because of the front (1) and because the south of England is further south (1). The south of England is in an area of high pressure which brings warm conditions in August (1). Since the isobars are closer together in the north of Scotland the wind speeds are higher than in the south of England (1). The south of England is dry whereas the north of Scotland has rain because the cold front is close to the north of Scotland (1).   **4**

Question 5

Upland Limestone: if Industry/Recreation and tourism chosen:

Areas of the Yorkshire Dales are used for the extraction of limestone which leaves large unsightly scars on the landscape (1), e.g. Swinden Quarry (1). The quarries can be dangerous if tourists stray into these areas (1). Tourists cannot access these areas as entry is restricted (1). There is a lot of pollution in the air from dust and traffic (1). Slow moving quarry traffic can cause congestion on country roads which could frustrate tourists (1). The processing of certain rocks needs fine grinding to separate out impurities and involves the dumping of large amounts of waste in artificial lagoons which causes visual pollution (1). Noise pollution is caused by both the heavy lorries transporting the limestone, and the sirens which warn of blasting events (2).   **4**

> *HINT* Make sure you do not just list land users who would be in conflict with each other. You must chose two groups then give the ways in which they conflict. Try to use a case study you have studied to give actual examples.

Upland Limestone: if Farming/Industry chosen:

Blasting is used to quarry limestone in the Yorkshire Dales and the noise from the blast could disturb farm animals (1) and cause sheep to miscarry their lambs (1). The dust resulting from blasting the rock settles on the fields and crops do not grow as well (1). The dust and the waste gets washed into the fields causing water pollution which makes the streams unsuitable for animals to drink from (1). The large, heavy lorries block the narrow country lanes which can prevent farmers from moving equipment, animals and products (1).   **4**

Rivers and Valleys: if Forestry/Recreation and tourism chosen:

Tourists complain that forestry does not look natural (1) and that trees interrupt views of rivers (1). When the trees are cut down the valley sides can looks unsightly (1), and the heavy machines can cause traffic problems (1). Access for walkers can be restricted (1). Careless tourists/campers may light fires which get out of control and cause damage and loss of forestry (1). Trail bikes and off-road vehicles can damage saplings (1).   **4**

Question 6

a) Areas with the highest life expectancy (over 77 years) include the UK (1) and Scandinavia (1). The areas with the lowest life expectancy are developing countries such as the Democratic Republic of the Congo (1). Most of Africa south of the Sahara desert has a life expectancy of below 63 years (1). Libya and Tunisia have the highest life expectancy of up to 64 years (1). Bolivia has the lowest life expectancy in South America at about 68 years (1).   **4**

> *HINT* Try to quote figures and name a country in your answer.

b) Life expectancy is higher in developed countries because there is better health care to treat illnesses (1). Poorer countries have endemic diseases like malaria which are debilitating and reduce life expectancy (1). Developed countries have advanced medical services which are easy to access, e.g. the UK has the NHS (1), and drugs to keep people healthier for longer (1). Medical checkups can identify possible problems and appropriate treatment can be given (1). Most people have access to clean water which reduces the spread of disease (1); good housing conditions prevent respiratory illnesses which can lead to long-term ill health (1). Developed countries have enough food to keep the population healthy (1), whereas people in developing countries have diets which are low in calories and/or protein which can result in diseases like kwashiorkor (1).   **6**

> ***HINT*** Remember to give reasons for the difference, do not simply describe the causes or list the reasons. Write in sentences – the more detail in an answer the more marks awarded.

Question 7

> ***HINT*** Using actual figures in your answer will gain you extra marks. Do not simply describe each pyramid, you need to make comparisons. Do not explain the differences – you will get no marks for this.

There are less dependent children in 2031 (1). There are fewer babies being born, the 0–4 age group drops from 330,000 to 250,000 (1). The largest age group in 1991 was the 25–29 year olds, whereas in 2031 the largest group is the 60–64 year olds (1). There are more people in the 80–84 age group (1), with females increasing from 75,000 to 100,000 (1).   **4**

Question 8

> ***HINT*** You need to give reasons why the land uses are in the rural/urban fringe, you will get no marks for description. Try to give actual examples from a case study you have studied. You can use the land uses in the question, plus add other land uses you might have studied. Do not repeat the same reason twice, e.g. land is cheaper – you will only get credit once.

Land is cheaper in the rural/urban fringe so houses can be bigger (1) and have gardens and garages (1). There is easy access to main roads (1) so it is easy to commute to work in the city (1). Out-of-town shopping centres and retail parks are attracted by the large available space (1) which can be used for expansion if needed (1) and for providing large car parks (most workers and customers arrive by car) (1). There are usually good road links for transport of goods in and out (1), as most goods are moved by lorry (1), and for workers and customers to access these areas (1). They are close to housing areas which provide a workforce and a market (2). Rates and rents are lower than in the city centre so shops can be bigger (1). The environment is attractive with little pollution (1).   **6**

Question 9

> ***HINT*** Apart from describing trends, try to put specific figures from the graph into your answer.

a) The average global temperature has risen constantly since 1880 (1) by around 1 degree (1). Apart from a small decrease between 1910 and 1915 (1), it rose gradually until 1945, when there was there was a peak (1). From around 1945 to 1965 there was very little overall increase in temperature (1) but since 1970 the increase has been faster (1).   **4**

b) Increasing global temperatures could make it too hot to grow certain crops (1). Droughts could reduce the amount of water available for irrigation (1) and result in more droughts in areas like Ethiopia (1). Climate change is also likely to cause stronger storms and more floods, which can damage crops (1). Higher temperatures and changing rainfall patterns could help some types of weeds and pests to spread to new areas (1). Warmer temperatures can lead to melting ice caps (1), which can cause a rise in sea levels (1) this could lead to flooding in low-lying areas such as the Netherlands (1). Warmer global temperatures could also change the habitats of many different species of wildlife (1).   **6**

> *HINT*   The question is about explanation. Describe the effect then explain the results of the change.

Question 10

a) Temperatures are much higher in the rainforest (1) and it is much wetter (1). The highest temperature in the rainforest is 29°C whereas in the tundra it is 10°C (1), a difference of 19°C (1). The range of temperature in the rainforest is 3°C, while it is 37°C in the tundra (1). The wettest month in the rainforest is April, with 210 mm of precipitation, whereas the wettest months in the tundra are July and August at 25mm (2).   **4**

> *HINT*   Apart from describing trends, use the figures in the graph in your answer. Make sure you take time to read the question. The negative figures in this question show that trees are being planted!

b) Laws put in place to protect the remaining areas of forest (1), e.g. make areas into National Parks (1). Employ rangers to patrol areas preventing illegal logging (1). Large fines for illegal logging (1). Conservation of areas must take into account the needs of the local people (1). The indigenous people should be involved in its protection as they know the forest and have an interest in protecting it and its wildlife (1). Large companies developing the rainforest are required to return the area to its natural state by replanting (1). Logging in a sustainable manner protects the environment but still produces money for the country (1). Give developing countries a reasonable price for their wood to ensure development of the area can take place and so reduce the need to cut down more trees (2).   **6**

> *HINT*   Your answer must include reference to both people and the environment. Do not describe the problems, explain solutions to the problems.

Question 11

a) Tropical storms occur in areas where the sea temperatures are over 27°C (1). They are found in areas which are between 30 degrees north and 30 degrees south of the Equator (1). They generally move in a westerly direction (1). Tropical cyclones occur in the Atlantic region and affect the Caribbean and USA (1). Tropical storms occur in various parts of the Pacific Ocean (1) and can affect the coastal regions of Mexico, southeast Asia, northeast Australia and the south Pacific islands (2). Some storms form in the Indian Ocean (1) and can affect India, Bangladesh, northwest Australia, some parts of east Africa and islands in the Indian Ocean such as Mauritius and Madagascar (2).   **4**

> *HINT*   Use the information on the map to describe the distribution. Name specific areas/countries in your answer. You do not need to give an explanation.

b) Hurricane Katrina caused widespread flooding along the Gulf Coast of America (1), forcing people to evacuate their homes (1). Homes were destroyed by the high winds and flooding (1). Levees burst, destroying farmland and leaving the people without food (1). Protected turtle nests were destroyed by the high tides (1). Trees were knocked down and destroyed (1). The high winds destroyed everything in their path, leaving thousands of people homeless (1). Many people were injured and diseases spread (1). Power lines, bridges and roads were destroyed (1).   **6**

> **HINT** In this question do not describe the effects of the storm. It needs explanation – you need to mention both the people and the environment. Refer to an example you have studied.

Question 12

> **HINT** Describe trends as well as using individual figures from the graph.

a) Overall the growth of world trade and GDP between 2005 and 2013 fluctuated (1). From 2005 to 2006, there was an increase of roughly 2% in exports (1) and a marginal increase in GDP (1). Between 2006 and 2009, there was a drastic decrease in the percentage of exports, from about 8% down to -12% (1). GDP also decreased between 2006 and 2009 by roughly 7% (1). Both exports and GDP rose considerably from 2009 to 2010, roughly a 26% and a 6% rise, respectively (1). Between 2010 and 2012, the percentage of exports fell once again by about 12% (1), but 2013 exports shows a final rise to about 4% (1). GDP gradually decreased between 2010 and 2013 from roughly 4% to 2% (1).   **4**

b) Some countries have better access to education (1) and therefore have a skilled workforce (1). Trade alliances, such as the EU, create trade barriers for countries outside the Union (1) making it more difficult for countries outside the Union to trade (1). Some countries only trade in primary goods so receive less money in return (1), while other countries have the technology to manufacture goods and sell them for a higher price and so become richer (1). Countries which rely on primary products are more vulnerable to price changes and market demand (1) and can find themselves with nothing to trade and/or can make very little profit (1). They are then forced to borrow money and end up in debt (1). They then may have to borrow money to pay the debt, limiting their chances of development (1) and the chance to trade in the higher priced manufactured goods (1).   **6**

> **HINT** Remember to explain not describe.

Question 13

a) Tourist spending doubled between 1992 and 2011 (1) from $50billion to $100 billion (1). Spending increased steadily until 2000 (1) by $28billion (1). It decreased for the next two years, 2001/2002, (1) by around $3billion (1). It rose steadily again until 2008 (1), when it reached $98billion (1). By 2009, it had decreased to around $90billion (1) before rising to its highest at over $100 billion in 2011 (1). Earnings for California rose from $18billion in 1992 to $30 billion in 2011 (1). Employment rose from 775,000 in 1992 to 900,000 in 2011 (1). In general employment falls when tourist spending falls (1). **4**

> **HINT** Use the information on the graph to describe the changes in tourism.

b) Eco-tourism aims to minimise the impact of tourism on an area (1). It promotes responsible travel to natural areas, conserves the environment (1) and improves the welfare of local people (1). It provides financial benefits to local people (1), e.g. jobs as tour guides (1), and gives them some control over developments in their home area (1). It raises awareness of the natural environment (1) and the culture of the area (1). Some of the money raised from this type of tourism is used for conservation of the area and its people's way of life (1). Eco-tourism tries to ensure that the tourists have a positive experience without negatively affecting the local people and the environment (1). **6**

> **HINT** Try to relate the question to an area you have studied. Mention examples in your answer.

Question 14

a) The largest number of episodes are found in Africa (1). India has a large number of cases (1), between 0.31 to 0.40 per child per year (1). Chad, Sudan and Bangladesh have some of the highest episodes (1), over 0.41 per child per year (1). China, South Africa and Mexico have around 0.21–0.30 (1). The least number of child episodes are in the developed areas (1), e.g. North America and Europe (1). **4**

> **HINT** Describe trends as well as naming specific areas/countries.

b) *Causes*:

AIDS is caused by the transfer of fluids from an infected person during unprotected sex (1). Sharing needles with a carrier can also pass on the disease (1). Some babies are born with AIDS, having been infected in the womb (1) or they can become infected through breast milk (1). In some countries there is a lack of education on how AIDS is spread (1). Having many different sexual partners (1). Infection from contaminated blood (1).

> **HINT** For full marks you need to refer to both causes and strategies.

Strategies:

Education campaigns promoting the benefits of safe sex (1) and the dangers of sharing hypodermic needles (1). Encouraging the use of condoms (1). Drug rehabilitation projects (1). Attempts to develop an AIDS vaccine (1). Needle exchange programmes (1). Blood screening (1). **6**

[END OF MARKING SCHEME]

Exam C Marking Scheme

Question 1

a) Corrie = 995409

Pyramidal peak = 992416

Arête = 998438 **3**

b) Snow collected in north-facing hollows turned to ice (1). This ice eroded the mountain on all sides creating corries (1). The back walls of the corries were eroded back towards each other (1) by the processes of plucking and abrasion (1) until a narrow knife-like ridge was formed between them (1). An arête was formed where two corries formed back to back (1). **4**

 Always try to include a diagram(s) in your answer. A simple sequence of diagrams can gain a mark. A full, detailed, annotated diagram(s) can achieve full marks.

Question 2

a) Pothole = 861681

Limestone pavement = 902647

Disappearing stream = 894657 **3**

b) During the Ice Age glaciers travelled over areas of carboniferous limestone, scraping away the surface and leaving them bare (1). Joints formed in the limestone as it dried out (1) and pressure was released (1). These joints or lines of weakness are more susceptible to chemical weathering than the surrounding limestone (1). The limestone is dissolved by rainwater, a weak carbonic acid (1), leaving deep gaps called grykes and raised blocks called clints. **4**

 Always try to include a diagram(s) in your answer. A simple sequence of diagrams can gain a mark. A full, detailed, annotated diagram(s) can achieve full marks.

A sample answer for the formation of stalactites and stalagmites:

Stalactites and stalagmites form in limestone caves or caverns where water drips from the ceiling (1). The water that seeps down through the limestone is loaded with dissolved lime (calcium carbonate) (1). When the water drips down from a cave roof a small amount of water will evaporate (1) and leave a tiny deposit of calcite ($CaCO_3$) (1). This is repeated every time water drips from the roof, so that in time a stalactite is formed (1). This looks like an icicle hanging from the ceiling (1). In a similar way calcite is deposited on the floor of the cave (1). As the drips land, the deposits build up to form a stalagmite (1). The splash spreads the calcite so stalagmites are thicker than stalactites (1). A stalagmite is a stumpy column of limestone sticking up from the floor of a cave (1). Rock pillars form where stalactites and stalagmites meet (1). **4**

Question 3

> **HINT** Remember to back up your answer with evidence from the OS map. Make use of grid references to identify specific points.

If map Item A is chosen:

Most settlement is along the coast where the land is low and flat for building (1), e.g. the town of Brodick at 015358 (1), and where there are beaches as development here may encourage tourists (1). Due to its coastal location, harbours and quays have developed for fishing (1). Most of the land is high and mountainous so no settlements are found there (1). The roads avoid the high lands and are mainly found in the flat land along the coast where it is easier to build (2). Where there is gently sloping lower ground, farming may be arable or mixed (1), e.g. 012373 (1), whereas on the steeper slopes and higher ground there will be livestock grazing due to the difficulty of using machinery here (2). Woodland is grown on land which is too high and cold for crops, such as 015395 (1). **5**

Question 4

> **HINT** Although it may be necessary to describe the weather conditions the marks will come from the explanation of the conditions.

There is an area of high pressure over Spain (1). High pressure systems bring low temperatures in winter and this is reflected as Madrid has a temperature of -5°C (2). The isobars are far apart so wind speeds are low (1). Spain also has obscured sky as fog is common in anti-cyclones (1). There are no fronts over Spain so there is no rainfall (1). **4**

Question 5

Glaciated Landscapes: if Recreation and tourism/Renewable energy chosen:

Glaciation produces high, steep mountains and deep valleys which create dramatic views encouraging sightseers, e.g. Helvellyn in the Lake District (1). The corrie sides and steep back walls provide opportunities for rock climbing (1). Arêtes encourage walkers, as they give them access to summits (1) and the variety of height and slopes allows different challenges for walkers and mountaineers (1). Skiing and snowboarding is possible in the corries as the snow lies in the north–facing basins (1). Glaciated areas are high and exposed making them suitable for the creation of wind power (1). Many of these areas are remote so the turbines will not disturb local communities (1). Winds are often more common in these areas, with higher wind speeds, making them particularly suitable for wind power (1). **4**

> **HINT** You will have studied two landscapes – choose the one you feel you have the most knowledge about. Make sure you choose appropriate land uses from the diagram – most land uses can be chosen but some are easier to answer than others. Also try to use specific examples in your answers. Do not list sports etc. that can take place, you need to say why they are possible in your landscape.

Question 6

a) There is a bus station (1), main railway station (1), tourist information centre (1), museums (1), town hall (1) and churches (1), and transport routes meet in this square (1). **3**

> **HINT** Features of CBD's are similar. Learn what the features are then pick them from the OS map used. Remember churches should be plural.

b) 0228 is an area of new housing whereas 0727 is an older, urban area (1). 0228 has a varied street pattern with crescents and cul-de-sacs whereas 0727 is grid iron pattern (1). 0727 has large buildings and port industries while 0228 has smaller buildings which would be housing (1). Many main roads and a railway run through 0727 while only minor roads run through 0228 (1) meaning less noise and pollution in 0228 than 0727 (1). There is more access to the countryside and a golf course in 0228 whereas there is less open space around 0727 and a poorer quality environment (2). **5**

> **HINT** When answering this question the marks come from giving the differences. Do not simply describe the two areas.

Question 7

> You can find more detailed markers' comments for this question in the 'How your paper will be marked' section.

If Population per doctor chosen:

Countries with a low population per doctor are normally more developed which means they have a better health care system (1) and this means more doctors treating fewer patients (1). More developed countries have more money so can afford to invest in a health care system (1). **4**

> **HINT** The marks come from the explanation. You will get no marks for describing the indicator. You need to mention both indicators otherwise you will get a maximum of three marks.

If Percentage population employed in agriculture chosen:

Countries with a high percentage of people employed in agriculture are usually less developed. This means that the country has little money to invest in industry (1) and so fewer people are employed in industry (1). People earn lower wages as agricultural jobs are poorly paid (1) and therefore there is a low standard of living (1). **4**

If Life expectancy at birth chosen:

Countries with a high life expectancy at birth are usually more developed and so have the money to invest in health care (1). It reflects advances made in public health (1) as well as access to primary health care services (1). Countries with a higher life expectancy have laws protecting people from environmental hazards (1) and exposure to hazards in the work place (1). **4**

If Gross domestic product chosen:

The higher the GDP the richer the country; if the figure is high it suggests a country has a large number of productive industries producing goods (1). It also suggests that the service industry is well developed (1) including services such as hospital and schools (1). If the figure is low it suggests that the country has few industries and services and therefore a poor standard of living (1). **4**

Question 8

a) Developing countries have higher birth rates as children are needed to bring in money for the family (1). There is a lack of government care for the elderly so children are needed to look after family in old age (1). Many children still die so people have many children to ensure some survive (1), but death rates are falling so population increases rapidly (1). There is a lack of education on family planning (1).

In developed countries, the birth and death rates are much lower so the population grows much more slowly (1). There is money to invest in medical care thus reducing the death rate and ensuring children survive at birth (1). Children are expensive so the more children in a family the greater the financial burden (1). Women want careers so put off having children (1) or limit the number of children they have (1). Later marriages are more common which results in fewer children (1). Contraception/family planning is widely available (1).   **5**

> *HINT* You can mention facts about both the developed and developing country. Remember to give reasons for the differences, do not simply describe. Reverse statements such as 'there is a lack of contraception and family planning in developing countries', 'contraception and family planning is widely available in developed countries' will only be awarded one mark.

b) Countries such as China introduced a one child policy (1). Better education for women on contraception/family planning could be provided (1) as well as better education for women which would allow them to have a career (1). Incentives could be offered, for instance more tax relief, free education for first child etc. (1).   **3**

> *HINT* Try to put specific examples in your answer.

Question 9

a) Both global temperatures and carbon dioxide emissions have increased between 1880 and 2010 (1). Carbon dioxide emissions rose throughout the period, while temperatures fluctuated with peaks and troughs (1). There was a large drop in temperatures around 1910 (1). There was a peak in 1950 where it rose by 0.5°F over a ten year period (1) and then dropped by 0.5°F over the next 10 years (1). Global temperatures have risen by around 1.5°F (1) whilst carbon dioxide emissions have risen by 100 parts per million (1). Both carbon dioxide emissions and temperatures have risen much faster since 1980 (1).   **4**

> *HINT* Use the figures in the graph to make specific points. Try to identify trends as well.

b) **If Develop alternative energy sources is chosen:**

Clean energy technologies like wind and solar power produce energy without burning fossil fuels which create harmful gases leading to global warming (2). Other technologies reduce greenhouse gas emissions through energy efficiency or by capturing these gases before they can enter the atmosphere (2). Solar energy is clean, producing no harmful emissions to add to the problem (1) and people who have solar panels on their homes buy less electricity from their utility companies because they're producing some electricity on their own (1).   **6**

> *HINT* Do not describe the different methods that could be used. You need to take them one-by-one and explain the reasons why each would reduce global warming.

If More efficient energy use is chosen:

Turning off lights, electrical appliances and thermostats uses less energy and so burns fewer fossil fuels putting less carbon dioxide into the atmosphere (2). Ensuring houses are properly insulated reduces heat loss so there is less need to use extra energy to heat the house (1). Walking and cycling instead of using the car reduces damaging emissions (1). Using energy efficient appliances reduces energy use, thus reducing emissions (1).   **6**

If Slow population growth is chosen:

More people means more demand for oil, gas, coal and other fuels mined or drilled from below the Earth's surface (1). When burned these fuels release carbon dioxide (CO_2) into the atmosphere which traps warm air inside like a greenhouse (1). An increase in population means more demand for food resulting in more methane being produced by increased agricultural production (1). Increased population means increased demand for transport resulting in more gases being released into the atmosphere (1). In countries like Brazil land is cleared of trees to create land for settlement (1) leaving less trees to remove the carbon from the atmosphere and so increasing global warming (1).   **6**

Question 10

a) Between 1990 and 2005, deforestation increased in all three countries (1). Brazil increased the most from 1.7m to 2.2m (1), an increase of 500,000 acres (1). Peru's deforestation stayed about the same (1). From 2005 to 2011 the amount of deforestation decreased in Brazil (1) by 1.6m acres (1), the amount of deforestation increased slightly in Peru by 25,000 acres (1) and changed very little in 2011 (1). The amount of deforestation in Bolivia has increased continually between 1990 and 2011 (1) by 200,000 acres overall (1).   **4**

> *HINT* When a question asks for detail you need to use the figures in the graph to make specific points. Try to identify trends as well.

b) **If Rainforest chosen:**

   Benefits:

   In Brazil removing the rainforest frees up valuable land for housing and agriculture (1) which is needed to accommodate the increasing population and the higher demand for food (2). Roads like the Amazon Highway can be built through the forest increasing the opportunity for trade (1). Jobs are provided for local workers in road building, logging, agriculture, mining and construction therefore improving the local economy and standard of living (1). Another benefit is the generation of income (often in valuable foreign currency) when wood, minerals, and other resources are sold and which contributes to reducing the national debt (1). Scientific investigation into rainforest plants may provide new food sources and medicines (1).

> *HINT* For full marks you need to mention both benefits and problems. Refer to specific examples.

Problems:

Large areas of rainforest are being destroyed and areas like Rondonia have suffered a large amount of deforestation (1). The habitats of animals have been severely damaged and some animals are faced with extinction (1). Valuable plants, which are used for medicinal purposes, are destroyed and along with them possible cures for illnesses such as cancer (1). The burning of the forest adds to the greenhouse effect as when trees are burned the carbon emissions become trapped in the atmosphere (1). Soil erosion is more common as there are no trees to bind the soil together (1). **6**

Question 11

a) Most storms start off in the Atlantic Ocean around the Caribbean Sea (1). They generally move from the SE to the NW (1), crossing the Tropic of Cancer (1). Some head for the east coast of the USA (1) while others move further west across the Gulf of Mexico (1). **4**

> *HINT*   Use directions and named locations in your answer.

b) **Japanese Earthquake:**

The earthquake caused a tsunami (1). Cars, ships and buildings were swept away by the wall of water (1). A nuclear reactor plant was damaged (1). Thousands of people living near the Fukushima nuclear power plant had to be evacuated (1). A 10 metre wave struck Sendai, deluging farmland and sweeping cars across the airport's runway (1). Fires broke out in the centre of the city (1) and a ship carrying 100 people was swept away off the coast (1). A dam burst in the northeastern Fukushima prefecture, sweeping away homes (1). About four million homes in and around Tokyo suffered power cuts (1) and thousands of people were killed (1) or made homeless (1). **6**

> *HINT*   To get full marks you must give examples from a natural disaster you have studied.

Question 12

a) The UK's export trade with the Eurozone is predicted to continually decrease between 1999 and 2030 (1) by around 18% in total (1). Between 1999 and 2011 it decreased by 8% (1). Exports to the USA also show a decrease of around 3% (1) between 1999 and 2030 (1). Trade with the BRIC countries shows an increase between 1999 and 2030 (1) from 3% to 16% (1). Trade with China and India also show increases (1). A small percentage of trade takes place with Brazil which increases very slightly between 1999 and 2030 (1). **4**

> *HINT*   Use figures and dates from the diagram.

b) Fair trade guarantees farmers a living wage (1). It gives access to credit at fair prices reducing the debt cycle (1). Farmers are encouraged to look after the environment by growing organic produce (1), decreasing the need to pollute the environment with fertilizers and pesticides (1). Fair payments provide cooperative members with food and other products they need which reduces hunger (1). Housing cooperatives provide shelter thus reducing the number of slum dwellers (1). Money goes into the communities where it is invested in education and health care, thus improving living conditions (2). Cooperatives are providing health care services and health education programmes for their members (1) tackling HIV/AIDS (1). **6**

> *HINT* For full marks you should mention the economy, people and the environment.

Question 13

a) Between 1995 and 2012 tourist arrivals trebled (1), increasing by 4.54m (1). There was a steady increase until 2002 when there was a decrease (1). India's share of world tourism also trebled (1). Earnings from tourism has gone up from $2.58b in 1995 to $15.95b in 2012 (1), an increase of $13.37b (1). **4**

> *HINT* Quote figures and dates in your answer. Try to process the figures.

b) In Mallorca, the government is encouraging tourists to stay in rural areas, e.g. in Pollensa Old Town, to reduce pressure on the coastal area of Puerto Pollensa (1). The government is trying to limit the amount of development allowed along the coast (1). There is tighter control over the type and height of buildings (1). More sewage plants could be built to prevent sewage from being dumped directly in the sea (1). Laws could be passed to prohibit the dropping of litter (1) punishable by fines (1). Pass by-laws ensuring live music stops at midnight (1). A green card has been created in the Balearics to encourage green tourism (1) and, for 10 Euros, tourists get discounts on visits to natural areas, cultural areas etc. (1). Under EU regulations, clean beaches can be awarded a Blue Flag (1). **6**

> *HINT* Refer to a specific case study in your answer: this shows the examiner your knowledge and marks are gained from detail.

Question 14

a) The incidence of heart attacks in both males and females in Scotland is much higher than in England (1). The rate for men in Scotland dropped more than males in England (1), to around 250 per 100,000 by 2007 (1). The incidence in women in Scotland fell faster than in England (1). By 2009/2010, the trend in women in England was still falling whereas in Scotland it had levelled off (1). **4**

> *HINT* Read the question carefully - the marks in this question come from describing the differences not from describing the individual trends.

b) **If Heart disease is chosen:**

Causes:

Eating too many fatty foods increases cholesterol levels (1) and this narrows the arteries increasing the chance of heart disease (1). Fatty foods lead to obesity which puts an extra strain on the heart (1). Lack of exercise raises blood pressure affecting the efficiency of the heart (1). Smoking narrows the arteries (1) and puts pressure on the heart (1). Stress increases blood pressure (1). Heart complaints can be hereditary (1).

Methods to combat the disease:

More people now have regular check-ups for cholesterol and blood pressure (1) allowing early intervention for at-risk patients (1). More advanced medical equipment is being invented and used (1), e.g. artificial heart valves (1), more advanced surgery is now available (1), e.g. bypass surgery (1). The government runs many campaigns to educate the public (1), e.g. stop smoking and healthy eating campaigns (1). People are encouraged to eat more healthily and take more exercise (1). Healthy eating is encouraged in school dining halls (1). Free and reduced membership of gyms can encourage people to exercise (1). **6**

 Do not just list the causes, you need to explain the problems created by them. For full marks you need to give some ways to combat the disease.

If Malaria is chosen:

Causes:

Malaria is spread by the female anopheles mosquito (1). The mosquito breeds in areas where temperatures are above 23°C (1) and areas of still, stagnant water are present (1). Malaria is caused when a human is bitten by the female anopheles mosquito (1) and a parasite is passed into the bloodstream (1). A mosquito can also pick up the parasite from an infected human (1) and then pass it on when it bites someone else (1).

Methods to combat the disease:

Use of insecticides to destroy the eggs (1), e.g. malathion (1). Use of anti-malarial drugs (1), e.g. chloroquine (1). Water released from dams to drown immature larvae (1). Scientists could use genetic engineering to produce sterile male mosquitoes (1). Breeding areas are drained (1). Planting eucalyptus trees to soak up moisture (1). Use of small fish to eat larvae (1). Mustard seeds to drag larvae below surface to drown them (1). The use of bed nets (1). Educating people on the spread of malaria (1). **6**

[END OF MARKING SCHEME]